THE PENGUIN CLASSICS

FOUNDER EDITOR (1944–64): E. V. RIEU

FRIEDRICH NIETZSCHE was born near Leipzig in 1844, the son of a Lutheran clergyman. He attended the famous Pforta School, then went to university at Bonn and at Leipzig, where he studied philology and read Schopenhauer. When he was only twenty-four he was appointed to the chair of classical philology at Basel University; he stayed there until his health forced him into retirement in 1879. While at Basel he made and broke his friendship with Wagner, participated as an ambulance orderly in the Franco-Prussian War, and published *The Birth of Tragedy* (1872), *Untimely Meditations* (1873–6) and the first two parts of *Human, All Too Human* (1878–9). From 1880 until his final collapse in 1889, except for brief interludes, he divorced himself from everyday life and, supported by his university pension, he lived mainly in France, Italy and Switzerland. The third part of *Human, All Too Human* appeared in 1880, followed by *The Dawn* in 1881. *Thus Spoke Zarathustra* was written between 1883 and 1885, and his last completed books were *Ecce Homo*, an autobiography, and *Nietzsche contra Wagner*. He became insane in 1889 and remained in a condition of mental and physical paralysis until his death in 1900.

R. J. HOLLINGDALE was born in London in 1930. He works on the *Guardian*. Among his many translations are two books by Nietzsche done in collaboration with Walter Kaufmann of Princeton University, and *Beyond Good and Evil*, *Thus Spoke Zarathustra*, Goethe's *Elective Affinities* and Schopenhauer's *Essays and Aphorisms* for the Penguin Classics. He is also the author of *Nietzsche: the Man and his Philosophy*, a study of Thomas Mann, a volume on Nietzsche in the Routledge Author Guides series and *A Nietzsche Reader*.

FRIEDRICH NIETZSCHE

Twilight of the Idols
AND
The Anti-Christ

TRANSLATED,
WITH AN INTRODUCTION AND
COMMENTARY, BY

R. J. Hollingdale

PENGUIN BOOKS

Penguin Books Ltd, Harmondsworth, Middlesex, England
Penguin Books, 625 Madison Avenue, New York, New York 10022, U.S.A.
Penguin Books Australia Ltd, Ringwood, Victoria, Australia
Penguin Books Canada Ltd, 2801 John Street, Markham, Ontario, Canada L3R 1B4
Penguin Books (N.Z.) Ltd, 182–190 Wairau Road, Auckland 10, New Zealand

—

Götzen-Dämmerung first published 1889
Der Antichrist first published 1895
This translation published 1968
Reprinted 1969, 1971, 1972, 1974, 1975, 1977, 1978, 1979, 1981

—

Translation copyright © R. J. Hollingdale, 1968
All rights reserved

—

Made and printed in Great Britain
by Hazell Watson & Viney Ltd,
Aylesbury, Bucks
Set in Monotype Garamond

CONTENTS

INTRODUCTION

Why read Nietzsche?

WHY read a book by Nietzsche – not to speak of two books? There are, after all, many other books to read, there are also many other things to do besides read. . . .

'Nothing', Nietzsche wrote in *Dawn* (in aphorism 18), 'has been purchased more dearly than the little bit of reason and sense of freedom which now constitutes our pride.' In a draft for the preface to his uncompleted *Will to Power* he wrote: 'A book for *thinking*, nothing more . . . ' This is one reason for reading Nietzsche's books: they are a unique course in thinking – nothing more, but also nothing less. Independence of mind, independence in general, was his greatest passion, and independence is above all what he teaches: not primarily a new set of ideas, or a new science, but philosophy in the proper and traditional sense of the word, a stimulation of the mind into activity, into becoming productive, into becoming airborne.

And that little bit of human reason we have is not only dearly bought, it is also easily lost. I think we are in some danger of actually losing it unless we remind ourselves constantly how little mankind would have left to be proud of if it lost its reason. There are even those who believe it is in their interest it should be lost, or at any rate reduced and held in check, though they couldn't be more wrong unless they are definitely *misanthropos* and hate mankind. But everywhere in the active world today intelligence is on the defensive; it has to fight to survive. For what characterizes the present age, the present decade? An excess of emotion, a constant stimulation of the emotions and a desire to have them stimulated more; nationalism and anti-nationalism, not for 'reasons' but as purely emotional reflexes; 'ideologies' which are likewise a transparent covering for the stupidest passions, greeds and resentments; 'hatred' (of war for instance) and 'love' (of peace for instance) as ultimate arguments, though they are so far from being arguments at all that a single emotional experience can reverse that polarity and turn a negative into a positive overnight; and in the private world a continual resort to the feelings, not as a reaction to an over-strict upbringing, which was the excuse of the twenties – who now living had an over-strict upbringing? – but as a flight from the brain to the 'heart' and then further on down; the desire to become the prisoner of some emotion presenting itself as a demand for more freedom; a 'cult of sensibility' which believes the opposite of feeling is 'being dead', whereas its true opposite is thinking (no wonder we have such a feeling for the eighteenth century: I am surprised *Clarissa* isn't a nightly television serial). There are no doubt reasons for this denigration of reason: the H-bomb is said to be the most important reason. ... Meanwhile, there has never in all history been so much *music*; it sometimes seems as if intelligence were being dissolved in rhythm. Nietzsche's books are, among other things, a protective against this dissolution.

To think well, to think at all: a third reason for reading Nietzsche would be to think *differently*. It is very hard to come to a rational opinion on any single subject: one does not think deeply enough or long enough; one has insufficient data, one makes up one's mind much too soon. Some feel they *ought* to have an opinion about this or that and go in search of one, and find one, from a sense of duty. Some become *committed* when very young and then find all their opinions perfectly natural, as a train leaving King's Cross committed to Aberdeen finds it perfectly natural to arrive in Aberdeen and not in Bombay. Some cannot bear uncertainty and therefore seek certainty and find it too quickly. Others perhaps admire someone and adopt his opinions so as to be more like him. Many opinions are merely a colouring induced by immediate environment, like a sunburn or a city pallor. There are indeed a thousand ways of acquiring an opinion that have nothing to do with rational thinking. Now Heaven forbid I should suggest that Nietzsche's opinions are the only rational opinions and that everyone should adopt them forthwith. That would be a very sad result of reading him and quite beside the point. To read Nietzsche, decisively to reject him, *and to know why* – that would be more to the point. More to the point still would be to see why he *could* be right, to see out of what mode of thinking such opinions as his can proceed, to see how many ways of thinking there are: in brief, to stop being parochial. Not knowing how to think true more than one sort of opinion is like never leaving the street one was born in.

Two alliterative examples of how Nietzsche may assist towards considering a subject from more than one viewpoint: decadence and democracy. *Décadence* (Nietzsche always uses the French word) is the common, perhaps also obsessive theme of both the books in this volume. He finds it everywhere; it lies behind all our valuations. No need to 'agree' here: one should rather be stimulated to ask 'what *is* decadence?' There are in our society people who are obviously decadent in the sense of degenerate: they require 'stronger and stronger and more and more frequent stimulants' to give them the feeling of being alive. But what about those who profit from exploiting this degeneracy; and those who hope to profit from attacking and abusing it? Are they too *'décadents'*? And what is one to say of a society in which sensual stimulation has to become stronger and stronger in order to produce the same effects; in which 'fashion' in every sense has to change almost with the moon in order to stay fashionable, that is to say in order still to be able to attract attention? Is modern 'tolerance' something positive, or is it a lack of interest, a lack of ability for self-defence against the new and possibly harmful? Is our society, in fact, 'changing' or is it decadent? *Democracy:* Nietzsche is known to be anti-democratic and is thought in this to be perversely opposing the whole general movement of the modern world. No need to agree or disagree here either: when Nietzsche was criticized for his moral theories he replied by asking 'whether we have in fact become more moral', and we might likewise ask ourselves whether we have in fact become more democratic and whether we in fact want to. Do you consider every other man and woman your equal, in every respect, in any respect? What does political democracy *mean?* Is it separable from industrial democracy? Who really *rules?* (do you rule?) Are we any closer now to *cultural* democracy, to an actual equivalence of cultural capacity between man and man, than we were in 1888, when *Twilight of the Idols* and *The Anti-Christ* were written? (From tonight's T.V. programme: B.B.C. 1 – Dixon of Dock Green, the Val Doonican Show, Saturday Thriller: Intent to Kill; B.B.C. 2 – Rilke on Rodin. Is it two different tastes or two different *species* which are being catered for here?) How much *social* democracy is there: in England, in Zambia, in Leningrad, in Boston, Massachusetts? Do you want total democracy (to paraphrase Dr Goebbels) or do you think we have sufficient or do you want less? Or don't you want anything very much? None of these questions can be answered by Nietzsche, but he *can* suggest that there are ways of considering them which have not yet occurred to you. And so for a hundred 'questions', some practical some theoretical, the answers to which are no more decided now than they were eighty years ago.

Philosopher and Stylist

Nietzsche is a philosopher and he writes about the traditional subjects of western philosophy: the problems of being and becoming, of appearance and reality, of determinism and freedom, of causation, of ethics, of aesthetics, of linguistics, of logic, of other philosophers. He is a psychologist and writes about the problems of human behaviour. He is a critic and writes about the arts, mainly literature and music. He is a philologist and classicist and writes about the life and letters of Greece and Rome. On none of the topics he treats does he fail to have something of interest to say, and generally his views are original and stimulating. His historical importance is very considerable: he comes at the end of the great line of German philosophers inaugurated by Leibniz and he anticipates the thought of the twentieth century in literally hundreds of ways, as well as anticipating the history of this century in a quite remarkable way. He is a philosopher for philosophers, but he is to a far greater degree than any of the other great philosophers also a philosopher for non-philosophers. This is partly the effect of his literary quality, partly that of the 'open' texture of his books. He moves from one subject to another ('quick in, quick out') often without any transition, never writing more than will express the idea he wishes to express, never trying to 'build' by applying putty, until he has produced, not a 'building' or system, but as it were an open network or grid of interlocking ideas. There is a full intellectual reality behind Nietzsche's brief aphorisms and chapters, but he presents it in assimilable quantities. This method of presentation is adhered to even in an apparently connected work like *The Anti-Christ*, and it is brilliantly exemplified in all its forms – the short aphorism, the long aphorism, the chain of aphorisms and the short chapter – in *Twilight of the Idols*.

The adoption of these short forms was in part, of course, dictated by the nature of his ideas, but it was also dictated by the nature of his style. Nietzsche's tendency as a writer of prose was to simplify the syntax of a language often Gothic in its shapelessness; to reduce the number of words needed to express a given idea; to shorten sentences so that none remains which cannot be uttered in a single breath; to invent metaphors both dramatic and obvious in meaning (the common tendency in even the best German writers was to turn every metaphor into an allegory): in brief, to give to the writing of German prose the kind of attention devoted to poetry. The result of these efforts is that Nietzsche is the greatest prose stylist in German and one of the very few whose pages can survive comparison with those of the great Roman and French stylists or with those of Swift, Gibbon, Henry James or Shaw. He has this too in common with Swift: anger does not make him verbose, it makes him *rapid*. His whole inclination, indeed, is towards speeding up the pace of German prose, and this makes him concise, brief and aphoristic. The summit of his achievement was reached in 1888, the year of *Twilight* and *The Anti-Christ*: in this year he really does achieve his 'ambition to say in ten sentences what everyone else says in a book – what everyone else *does not* say in a book'.

INTRODUCTION

Life

The year 1888 was indeed the climax of Nietzsche's life in every respect. The preceding decade had been very productive: in 1878 appeared *Human, All Too Human,* the first work in which his genius is clearly apparent; it was followed by *Assorted Opinions and Maxims* (1879), *The Wanderer and his Shadow* (1880), *Dawn* (1881), *The Gay Science* (1882, enlarged 1887), *Thus Spoke Zarathustra* (1883–5), *Beyond Good and Evil* (1886) and *Towards a Genealogy of Morals* (1887). During the latter half of this period he was also working on a large-scale undertaking to be called *The Will to Power,* the notes and sketches for which were subsequently published under that title and in a two-volume collection called *Die Unschuld des Werdens* (The Innocence of Becoming). In 1888 he abandoned *The Will to Power* and substituted *The Revaluation of all Values,* of which *The Anti-Christ* was originally intended to form the first part; in addition he produced five short books: *The Wagner Case, Twilight of the Idols, Ecce Homo, Nietzsche contra Wagner* and *Dithyrambs of Dionysus.* A productivity which had always been considerable became in 1888 enormous.

This year was also climactic in that the works written then constitute a self-epitome: his philosophy is complete and he is summing it up. *Twilight of the Idols* rehearses, with incomparable economy, most of the themes of the previous ten years; *The Anti-Christ* gathers together his scattered reflections and thoughts on the Christian religion and Christian morality and orders them in a single polemical essay into the explicit directness of which no sort of compromise or *arrière-pensée* is permitted to intrude.

And the year was climactic in being the last of his active life. He had been ill for about sixteen years as the consequence, almost certainly, of a syphilitic infection contracted when he was a student; in the first days of January 1889 he suffered a total mental collapse and though he lived on until August 1900 he wrote nothing more. The sense of mental excitement he experienced throughout 1888 is recorded in his letters rather than his books (except for *Ecce Homo,* where his habitual, and studied, self-advertisement is sometimes intensified into megalomania), but it undoubtedly contributed to the extreme urgency which characterizes his last style. This would not have surprised Nietzsche himself, since he was accustomed to think of artistic achievement as pathologically conditioned.

Nietzsche was born in Röcken, a village in Prussian Saxony, in 1844. His father and both grandfathers were Lutheran pastors and as a boy he was a pious believer. He attended Pforta school, the Rugby of Prussia, from 1858 to 1864, and then went to Bonn and subsequently Leipzig university (1864–9). At Bonn he studied theology but gave it up when he lost his religious faith; he continued as a student of philology and gained so great a reputation in it that he was appointed to the chair of classical philology at Basel university at the age of twenty-four before having obtained his doctorate, which was awarded him by Leipzig without examination. He taught at Basel for ten years (1869–79), becoming a Swiss to do so, and published his earliest books: *The Birth of Tragedy* (1872) and the four *Untimely Meditations* (1873–6). He also became a 'disciple' of Richard Wagner and devoted much time and energy to assisting in establishing the Bayreuth Festival, which was inaugurated in 1876. But by that time Nietzsche had come to think he had been mistaken in seeing in Wagner the new saviour of German art, and this disillusionment, combined with his sense that the newly-established *Reich* was a victory for philistinism, turned him against all things German and he became year by year more critical of the 'new Germany' (see 'What the Germans Lack' in *Twilight*).

In 1876 he began writing *Human, All Too Human*, and when it appeared in 1878 his breach with his past was complete. A year later he suffered an almost total collapse of health and was compelled to abandon his university career: for the next ten years he lived in a state of recurring ill-health which culminated in final collapse and insanity. During these years he wrote all his important books, living in lodgings and hotel rooms mainly in Switzerland and Italy. He was for that decade certainly one of the loneliest of men, though fundamentally he liked and needed solitude. He never married.

The Birth of Tragedy and the first of the *Untimely Meditations* won him a certain small notoriety, but his subsequent books fell dead from the press – only 170 copies of *Human, All Too Human* were sold during its first year – and from the fourth part of *Zarathustra* onwards he had to pay for their publication himself (which he could ill afford to do). Until the end of 1887, in spite of having produced a series of books without equal in the German literature of their time and now world-famous, he was virtually unknown. In 1888 he began to acquire a name: a few, mainly hostile articles were written about him in journals, and the Danish critic Georg Brandes lectured in Copenhagen on his works. But it was not until the 1890s that the public in Germany and abroad became aware of him, and then his reputation suddenly soared, so that by 1900 he was famous, not to say notorious. Of this he knew nothing, having become mentally a child again. Alone, ill and unsuccessful, Nietzsche in the 1880s is however not a figure to pity: in one book after another, couched in a style it must have been a perpetual delight to realize, he celebrated as no one else has ever done the splendour, power and joy of life.

Note on the Text

Götzen-Dämmerung, oder: Wie man mit dem Hammer philosophirt was published by C. G. Naumann of Leipzig in January 1889, a few weeks after Nietzsche's collapse. It was the last book Nietzsche himself saw printed. It was written between the end of June and the beginning of September 1888, with the fore-word, the chapter 'What the Germans Lack' and some of the 'Expeditions of an Untimely Man' added at the end of September, and it was printed by the end of October. The book originally bore the title 'Müssiggang eines Psycholo-gen' (A Psychologist's Leisure, or The Idle Hours of a Psychologist): this modest title was objected to by Nietzsche's enthusiastic admirer Peter Gast, who urged him to find some-thing more 'splendid'; Nietzsche acceded to this request with a parody of Wagner's *Götterdämmerung* (Twilight of the Gods). The change seems to have been made while the book was already being set up in type (the title page of the manuscript from which it was set is missing, indicating perhaps that Nietzsche had taken it back to make the alteration and that it was subsequently mislaid), and this explains a few otherwise puzzling references to the superseded title in the text.

Der Antichrist was written between 3 and 30 September 1888, immediately after the completion of *Twilight*. It was first intended as the first part of *The Revaluation of all Values*: a plan for that book which has been preserved reads: 'Revaluation of all Values. Book 1: The Anti-Christ. Attempt at a Critique of Christianity. Book 2: The Free Spirit. Critique of Philosophy as a Nihilistic Movement. Book 3: The Immoralist. Critique of the Most Fatal Kind of Ignorance, Morality. Book 4: Dionysus. Philosophy of Eternal Recurrence.' Nietzsche, it should be remarked, was *very* fond of composing plans for books: his posthumous papers include dozens of such plans, among them twenty-five different plans for the projected but unrealized *Will to Power* and several for books which exist only as plans; he also drew a number of title pages for ghostly books, with title, author and publisher neatly inked in and only the date of publication omitted. This being so, the above plan for the *Revaluation* does not *necessarily* imply a firm intention to carry it out, and no sooner in fact was *The Anti-Christ* completed than Nietzsche was referring to it in his letters as the *whole Revaluation:* this is in the autumn of 1888, when the impending catastrophe is beginning to cast its shadow before it and Nietzsche is almost hysterically anxious for the *Revaluation* to make its appearance in print and cannot contemplate waiting until he has written three more 'books' of the length of *The Anti-Christ*. He is already working on his self-proclamation *Ecce Homo* and is preparing *Nietzsche contra Wagner* as a follow-up to *The Wagner Case*, and he is determined to discharge every piece of artillery in his possession at the world's head in the New Year: *Anti-Christ* must therefore go out alone. It was ready for printing by the end of 1888 but was not in fact sent to Naumann; meanwhile all reference to the

Revaluation had been removed from its title. There are two manuscript title pages preserved: the earlier follows the above plan: *The Anti-Christ. Attempt at a Critique of Christianity. Book One of the Revaluation of all Values,* and was presumably written on 3 September. The later one reads: *The Anti-Christ. Revaluation of all Values*: but the sub-title has been crossed out and *A Curse on Christianity* substituted. As this last is written in the spiky hand characteristic of the first days of Nietzsche's insanity – no one familiar with his handwriting can be in any doubt on this point, so marked is the change it underwent after his collapse – it is probably better to leave *The Anti-Christ* without any sub-title. (I have gone into this question at some length in order to explain references to the *Revaluation* in the text of both *Twilight* and *The Anti-Christ.*) The book was first published in 1895, in volume VIII of the *Gesamtausgabe in Grossoktav* (Naumann, Leipzig); a small number of omissions from the text were subsequently published and are restored in Karl Schlechta's edition (*Werke in drei Bänden*, vol. II, 1955).

The title *Der Antichrist could* mean 'The Anti-Christian': the German for Christian is *Christ,* for Christ *Christus.* But when Nietzsche writes, in the 'Essay in Self-Criticism' prefaced to the 1886 edition of *The Birth of Tragedy*: '... wer wüsste den rechten Namen des Antichrist?' (who could know the rightful name of the Anti-Christ?), and in *Ecce Homo* (III 2): 'ich bin ... der *Antichrist*' (I am the *Anti-Christ*), he certainly means 'Anti-Christ' and not 'anti-Christian', and therefore that is what he means by the title of the most violent and violently-provocative of his polemics against Christianity.

Note on the Notes

As both the works included in this volume are short it seems inappropriate to bury them under a load of apparatus. However, in *Twilight* especially, what the reader has is a *compendium* of Nietzsche's philosophy and some help in using it is called for. Not everything is self-explanatory: Nietzsche sometimes employs phrases and coinages of his own in a way that presupposes an acquaintanceship with his previous books. One encounters, for example, 'the will to power', which is not strictly meaningful outside the context of Nietzsche's philosophy; and 'Dionysian', which does not mean here what it means elsewhere; and 'The will to a system is a lack of integrity', which seems to be a *non sequitur*. The usefulness of the book is increased, too, if its connexion with Nietzsche's work as a whole is indicated, however briefly: the reader will probably be interested to know what else Nietzsche had to say about this or that topic, this or that person. The commentary which seeks to satisfy some of these requirements is in the form of notes, which are divided into footnotes, appendices and a glossary of names. The last two divisions are still *notes* and retain the quality of notes: they are not offered as exhaustive accounts of Nietzsche's attitudes, and they are sent to the end of the book only because they are a little too long to be accommodated at the foot of the page.

21 *October* 1967   R.J.H.

TWILIGHT OF THE IDOLS
or How to Philosophize with
a Hammer

Foreword

To stay cheerful when involved in a gloomy and exceedingly responsible business is no inconsiderable art: yet what could be more necessary than cheerfulness? Nothing succeeds in which high spirits play no part. Only excess of strength is proof of strength. – *A revaluation of all values,** this question-mark so black, so huge it casts a shadow over him who sets it up – such a destiny of a task compels one every instant to run out into the sunshine so as to shake off a seriousness grown all too oppressive. Every expedient for doing so is justified, every 'occasion' a joyful occasion.† Above all, *war*. War has always been the grand sagacity of every spirit which has grown too inward and too profound; its curative power lies even in the wounds one receives. A maxim whose origin I withold from learned curiosity has long been my motto:

increscunt animi, virescit volnere virtus.‡

Another form of recovery, in certain cases even more suited to me, is to *sound out idols*. . . . There are more idols in the world than there are realities: that is *my* 'evil eye' for this world, that is also my 'evil ear'. . . . For once to pose questions here with a *hammer* and perhaps to receive for answer that famous hollow sound which speaks of inflated bowels – what a delight for one who has ears behind his ears – for an old psychologist and pied piper like me, in presence of whom precisely that which would like to stay silent *has to become audible* . . .

---

* See the Introduction, p. 15, for an explanation of this phrase.

† *jeder 'Fall' ein Glücksfall*. 'Fall' means case, 'Glücksfall' a piece of good luck. As well as being a play on words there seems to be a reference intended to *Der Fall Wagner* (The Wagner Case), Nietzsche's witty attack on Wagner completed immediately before *Twilight* was begun and which was also announced, ironically of course, as a 'relief' from a sterner task.

‡ The spirit grows, strength is restored by wounding.

This book too* – the title betrays it† – is above all a relaxation, a sunspot, an escapade into the idle hours of a psychologist. Perhaps also a new war? And are new idols sounded out? ... This little book is a *grand declaration of war;* and as regards the sounding-out of idols, this time they are not idols of the age but *eternal* idols which are here touched with the hammer as with a tuning fork – there are no more ancient idols in existence. ... Also none more hollow. ... That does not prevent their being the *most believed in*; and they are not, especially in the most eminent case, called idols ...

FRIEDRICH NIETZSCHE

Turin, 30 September 1888,
on the day the first book of the
Revaluation of all Values was
completed.

* Like *The Wagner Case*, presumably.
† See the Introduction, page 14.

Maxims and Arrows

1. Idleness is the beginning of all psychology. What? could psychology be – a vice?

2. Even the bravest of us rarely has the courage for what he really *knows* . . .

3. To live alone one must be an animal or a god – says Aristotle. There is yet a third case: one must be both – a *philosopher*.

4. 'All truth is simple.' – Is that not a compound lie? –

5. Once and for all, there is a great deal I do *not* want to know. – Wisdom sets bounds even to knowledge.

6. It is by being 'natural' that one best recovers from one's unnaturalness, from one's spirituality . . .

7. Which is it? is man only God's mistake or God only man's mistake? –

8. *From the military school of life.* – What does not kill me makes me stronger.

9. Help thyself: then everyone will help thee too. Principle of Christian charity.

10. Let us not be cowardly in face of our actions! Let us not afterwards leave them in the lurch! – Remorse of conscience is indecent.

11. Can an *ass* be tragic? – To be crushed by a burden one can neither bear nor throw off? . . . The case of the philosopher.

12. If we possess our *why* of life we can put up with almost any *how*. – Man does *not* strive after happiness; only the Englishman does that.

13. Man created woman – but what out of? Out of a rib of his God, of his 'ideal' . . .

14. What? you are seeking? you want to multiply yourself by ten, by a hundred? you are seeking followers? – Seek *noughts*! – *

15. Posthumous men – like me, for instance – are not so well understood as timely† men, but they are *listened to* better. More precisely: we are never understood – and *hence* our authority ...

16. *Among women*. – 'Truth? Oh, you don't know the truth, do you! Is it not an outrage on all our *pudeurs*?' –

17. This is an artist as an artist should be, modest in his requirements: there are only two things he really wants, his bread and his art – *panem et* Circen ...‡

18. He who does not know how to put his will into things at least puts a *meaning* into them: that is, he believes there is a will in them already (principle of 'belief').

19. What? you have chosen virtue and the heaving bosom, yet at the same time look with envy on the advantages enjoyed by those who live for the day? – But with virtue one *renounces* 'advantage' ... (laid at the door of an anti-Semite).

20. The complete woman perpetrates literature in the same way as she perpetrates a little sin: as an experiment, in passing, looking around to see if someone notices and *so that* someone may notice ...

21. To get into only those situations in which illusory virtues are of no use, but in which, like the tightrope-walker on his rope, one either falls or stands – or gets off ...

* *Suche Nullen!* 'Nullen' means nobodies, ciphers, as well as noughts – 'Seek *nobodies*!' The aphorism is a pun: 'if you want to multiply yourself by 100 [have followers] get noughts [nobodies] behind you!'

† *zeitgemässe*. Nietzsche's conception of himself as *unzeitgemäss* (untimely, inopportune, independent of the age) is reflected in the chapter title 'Expeditions of an Untimely Man' (*Streifzüge eines Unzeitgemässen*), which itself refers back to *Unzeitgemässe Betrachtungen* (Untimely Meditations), the collective title of the four essays published 1873–6 and intended for others left incomplete.

‡ bread and *Circe*, in place of *panem et circenses* = bread and circuses.

22. 'Bad men have no songs'.* – How is it the Russians have songs?

23. 'German spirit':† for eighteen years‡ a *contradictio in adjecto*.§

24. In order to look for beginnings one becomes a crab. The historian looks backwards; at last he also *believes* backwards.

25. Contentment protects one even from catching a cold. Has a woman who knew she was well dressed ever caught a cold? – I am assuming she was hardly dressed at all.

26. I mistrust all systematizers and avoid them. The will to a system is a lack of integrity.‖

27. Women are considered deep – why? because one can never discover any bottom to them. Women are not even shallow.

28. If a woman possesses manly virtues one should run away from her; and if she does not possess them she runs away herself.

29. 'How much the conscience formerly had to bite on!¶ what good teeth it had! – And today? what's the trouble?' – A dentist's question.

30. One seldom commits only one rash act. In the first rash act one always does too much. For just that reason one usually commits a second – and then one does too little . . .

* Refers to a popular adage deriving from Johann Gottfried Seume's poem *Die Gesänge*.

† *Geist*. All the meanings contained in this word cannot be conveyed in a single English word: what is meant is spirit, mind, intellect, intelligence. I have translated it as 'spirit', 'spiritual' when the most inclusive sense seems indicated, as 'intellect', 'intellectual' when this seems more appropriate.

‡ i.e. since the establishment of the *Reich*.

§ contradiction in terms.

‖ A note on Nietzsche's attitude towards philosophical systems will be found as Appendix A.

¶ *Gewissensbisse* (conscience-bites) is the ordinary term for pangs of conscience.

31. When it is trodden on a worm will curl up.* That is prudent. It thereby reduces the chance of being trodden on again. In the language of morals: *humility*. –

32. Hatred of lies and dissembling may arise out of a sensitive notion of honour; the same hatred may arise out of cowardice, in as much as lying is *forbidden* by divine command. Too cowardly to tell lies ...

33. How little is needed for happiness! The note of a bagpipe. – Without music life would be a mistake. The German even thinks of God as singing songs.†

34. *On ne peut penser et écrire qu'assis*‡ (G. Flaubert). – Now I have you, nihilist! Assiduity§ is the *sin* against the holy spirit. Only ideas *won by walking* have any value.

35. There are times when we are like horses, we psychologists, and grow restive: we see our own shadow moving up and down before us. The psychologist has to look away from *himself* in order to see at all.

36. Whether we immoralists do virtue any *harm*? – As little as anarchists do princes. Only since they have been shot at do they again sit firmly on their thrones. Moral: one must shoot at morals.

37. You run on *ahead*? – Do you do so as a herdsman? or as an exception? A third possibility would be as a deserter. ....
First question of conscience.

38. Are you genuine? or only an actor? A representative?

* *Der getretene Wurm krümmt sich* plays upon the German equivalent of 'Even a worm will turn'.

† Refers to the traditional misreading of a line in Ernst Moritz Arndt's patriotic song *Des deutschen Vaterland:* 'So weit die deutsche Zunge klingt, Und Gott im Himmel Lieder singt'. 'Gott' is dative: Wherever the German tongue resounds And sings songs to God in Heaven – but is humorously understood as nominative: And God in Heaven sings songs.

‡ One can think and write only when sitting down.

§ *das Sitzfleisch:* etymologically 'the posterior' (sitting-flesh). 'Assiduity', from *sedere* = to sit, is cognate. Hence the contrast with 'walking' ideas.

or that itself which is represented? – Finally you are no more than an imitation of an actor. . . . *Second* question of conscience.

39. *The disappointed man speaks.* – I sought great human beings, I never found anything but the *apes* of their ideal.

40. Are you one who looks on? or who sets to work? – or who looks away, turns aside. . . . *Third* question of conscience.

41. Do you want to accompany? or go on ahead? or go off alone? . . . One must know *what* one wants and *that* one wants. – *Fourth* question of conscience.

42. For me they were steps, I have climbed up upon them – therefore I had to pass over them. But they thought I wanted to settle down on them . . .

43. What does it matter that *I* am proved right! I *am* too much in the right. – And he who laughs best today will also laugh last.

44. Formula of my happiness: a Yes, a No, a straight line, a *goal* . . .

The Problem of Socrates

I

In every age the wisest have passed the identical judgement on life: *it is worthless*. ... Everywhere and always their mouths have uttered the same sound – a sound full of doubt, full of melancholy, full of weariness with life, full of opposition to life. Even Socrates said as he died: 'To live – that means to be a long time sick: I owe a cock to the saviour Asclepius'.* Even Socrates had had enough of it. – What does that *prove*? What does it *point to*? – Formerly one would have said (– oh, and did say, and loudly enough, and our pessimists† most of all!): 'Here at any rate there must be something true! The *consensus sapientium*‡ is proof of truth.' – Shall we still speak thus today? are we *allowed* to do so? 'Here at any rate there must be something *sick*' – this is *our* retort: one ought to take a closer look at them, these wisest of every age! Were they all of them perhaps no longer steady on their legs? belated? tottery? *décadents*? Does wisdom perhaps appear on earth as a raven which is inspired by the smell of carrion? ...

2

This irreverent notion that the great sages are *declining types* first dawned on me in regard to just the case in which learned and unlearned prejudice is most strongly opposed to it: I recognized Socrates and Plato as symptoms of decay, as agents of the dissolution of Greece, as pseudo-Greek, as anti-Greek (*Birth of Tragedy*, 1872).§ That *consensus sapientium* – I saw more

* According to Plato (*Phaedo*), Socrates' last words were: 'Crito, I owe a cock to Asclepius; will you remember to pay the debt?' One gave a cock to Asclepius on recovering from an illness: Socrates seems to be saying that life is, or his life has been an illness.

† Specifically the followers of Schopenhauer, among whom Nietzsche himself was numbered in his young days.

‡ Unanimity of the wise.   § Nietzsche's first published book.

and more clearly – proves least of all that they were right about what they were in accord over: it proves rather that they themselves, these wisest men, were in some way in *physiological* accord since they stood – *had* to stand – in the same negative relation to life. Judgements, value judgements concerning life, for or against, can in the last resort never be true: they possess value only as symptoms, they come into consideration only as symptoms – in themselves such judgements are stupidities. One must reach out and try to grasp this astonishing *finesse, that the value of life cannot be estimated.* Not by a living man, because he is a party to the dispute, indeed its object, and not the judge of it; not by a dead one, for another reason. – For a philosopher to see a problem in the *value* of life thus even constitutes an objection to him, a question-mark as to his wisdom, a piece of unwisdom. – What? and all these great wise men – they have not only been *décadents,* they have not even been wise? – But I shall get back to the problem of Socrates.

3

Socrates belonged, in his origins, to the lowest orders: Socrates was rabble. One knows, one sees for oneself, how ugly he was. But ugliness, an objection in itself, is among Greeks almost a refutation. Was Socrates a Greek at all? Ugliness is frequently enough the sign of a thwarted development, a development *retarded* by interbreeding. Otherwise it appears as a development in *decline.* Anthropologists among criminologists tell us the typical criminal is ugly: *monstrum in fronte, monstrum in animo.** But the criminal is a *décadent.* Was Socrates a typical criminal? – At least that famous physiognomist's opinion which Socrates' friends found so objectionable would not contradict this idea. A foreigner passing through Athens who knew how to read faces told Socrates to his face that he *was* a *monstrum* – that he contained within him every kind of foul vice and lust. And Socrates answered merely: 'You know me, sir!' –

* a monster in face, a monster in soul.

4

It is not only the admitted dissoluteness and anarchy of his instincts which indicates *décadence* in Socrates: the superfetation of the logical and that *barbed malice* which distinguishes him also point in that direction. And let us not forget those auditory hallucinations which, as 'Socrates' demon', have been interpreted in a religious sense. Everything about him is exaggerated, *buffo*, caricature, everything is at the same time hidden, reserved, subterranean. – I seek to understand out of what idiosyncrasy that Socratic equation reason = virtue = happiness derives: that bizarrest of equations and one which has in particular all the instincts of the older Hellenes against it.

5

With Socrates Greek taste undergoes a change in favour of dialectics: what is really happening when that happens? It is above all the defeat of a *nobler* taste; with dialectics the rabble gets on top. Before Socrates, the dialectical manner was repudiated in good society: it was regarded as a form of bad manners, one was compromised by it. Young people were warned against it. And all such presentation of one's reasons was regarded with mistrust. Honest things, like honest men, do not carry their reasons exposed in this fashion. It is indecent to display all one's goods. What has first to have itself proved is of little value. Wherever authority is still part of accepted usage and one does not 'give reasons' but commands, the dialectician is a kind of buffoon: he is laughed at, he is not taken seriously. – Socrates was the buffoon who *got himself taken seriously:* what was really happening when that happened?

6

One chooses dialectics only when one has no other expedient. One knows that dialectics inspire mistrust, that they are not very convincing. Nothing is easier to expunge than the effect of a dialectician, as is proved by the experience of every speech-making assembly. Dialectics can be only a *last-ditch weapon* in the hands of those who have no other weapon left. One must have to *enforce* one's rights: otherwise one makes no use of it. That is why the Jews were dialecticians; Reynard the Fox was a dialectician: what? and Socrates was a dialectician too? –

7

– Is Socrates' irony an expression of revolt? of the *ressentiment* of the rabble? does he, as one of the oppressed, enjoy his own form of ferocity in the knife-thrust of the syllogism? does he *revenge* himself on the aristocrats he fascinates? – As a dialectician one is in possession of a pitiless instrument; with its aid one can play the tyrant; one compromises by conquering. The dialectician leaves it to his opponent to demonstrate he is not an idiot: he enrages, he at the same time makes helpless. The dialectician *devitalizes* his opponent's intellect. – What? is dialectics only a form of *revenge* in the case of Socrates?

8

I have intimated the way in which Socrates could repel: it is therefore all the more necessary to explain the fact *that* he exercised fascination. – That he discovered a new kind of *agon,* that he was the first fencing-master in it for the aristocratic circles of Athens, is one reason. He fascinated because he touched on the agonal instinct of the Hellenes – he introduced a variation into the wrestling-matches among the youths and young men. Socrates was also a great *erotic.*

9

But Socrates divined even more. He saw *behind* his aristocratic Athenians; he grasped that *his* case, the idiosyncrasy of his case, was already no longer exceptional. The same kind of degeneration was everywhere silently preparing itself: the old Athens was coming to an end. – And Socrates understood that all the world had need of him – his expedient, his cure, his personal art of self-preservation. . . . Everywhere the instincts were in anarchy; everywhere people were but five steps from excess: the *monstrum in animo* was the universal danger. 'The instincts want to play the tyrant; we must devise a *counter-tyrant* who is stronger'. ... When that physiognomist had revealed to Socrates what he was, a cave of every evil lust, the great ironist uttered a phrase that provides the key to him. 'That is true,' he said, 'but I have become master of them all.' *How* did Socrates become master of *himself*? – His case was after all only the extreme case, only the most obvious instance of what had at that time begun to be the universal exigency: that no one was any longer master of himself, that the instincts were becoming mutually *antagonistic*. He exercised fascination as this extreme case– his fear-inspiring ugliness expressed it for every eye to see: he fascinated even more, it goes without saying, as the answer, as the solution, as the apparent *cure* for this case. –

10

If one needs to make a tyrant of *reason*, as Socrates did, then there must exist no little danger of something else playing the tyrant. Rationality was at that time divined as a *saviour;* neither Socrates nor his 'invalids' were free to be rational or not, as they wished– it was *de rigueur*, it was their *last* expedient. The fanaticism with which the whole of Greek thought throws itself at rationality betrays a state of emergency: one was in peril, one had only *one* choice: either to perish or – be *absurdly rational*. ... The moralism of the Greek philosophers from Plato downwards is pathologically conditioned: likewise their estimation of dialectics. Reason = virtue = happiness means merely: one must imitate Socrates and counter the dark desires by producing a permanent *daylight* – the daylight of reason. One must be prudent, clear, bright at any cost: every yielding to the instincts, to the unconscious, leads *downwards* ...

11

I have intimated the way in which Socrates exercised fascination: he seemed to be a physician, a saviour. Is it necessary to go on to point out the error which lay in his faith in 'rationality at any cost'?— It is self-deception on the part of philosophers and moralists to imagine that by making war on *décadence* they therewith elude *décadence* themselves. This is beyond their powers: what they select as an expedient, as a deliverance, is itself only another expression of *décadence* – they *alter* its expression, they do not abolish the thing itself. Socrates was a misunderstanding: *the entire morality of improvement, the Christian included, has been a misunderstanding*. . . . The harshest daylight, rationality at any cost, life bright, cold, circumspect, conscious, without instinct, in opposition to the instincts, has itself been no more than a form of sickness, another form of sickness – and by no means a way back to 'virtue', to 'health', to happiness. . . . To *have* to combat one's instincts – that is the formula for *décadence*: as long as life is *ascending*, happiness and instinct are one. –

12

– Did he himself grasp that, this shrewdest of all self-deceivers? Did he at last say that to himself in the *wisdom* of his courage for death? . . . Socrates *wanted* to die – it was not Athens, it was *he* who handed himself the poison cup, who compelled Athens to hand him the poison cup. . . . 'Socrates is no physician,' he said softly to himself: 'death alone is a physician here. . . . Socrates himself has only been a long time sick . . .'

'Reason' in Philosophy

I

You ask me about the idiosyncrasies of philosophers? ...
There is their lack of historical sense, their hatred of even the
idea of becoming, their Egyptianism. They think they are
doing a thing *honour* when they dehistoricize it, *sub specie
aeterni** – when they make a mummy of it. All that philosophers
have handled for millennia has been conceptual mummies;
nothing actual has escaped from their hands alive. They kill,
they stuff, when they worship, these conceptual idolaters –
they become a mortal danger to everything when they worship. Death, change, age, as well as procreation and growth,
are for them objections – refutations even. What is, does not
become; what becomes, *is* not.... Now they all believe, even
to the point of despair, in that which is. But since they cannot
get hold of it, they look for reasons why it is being withheld
from them. 'It must be an illusion, a deception which prevents
us from perceiving that which is: where is the deceiver to be
found?' – 'We've got it,' they cry in delight, 'it is the senses!
These senses, *which are so immoral as well,* it is they which deceive
us about the *real* world. Moral: escape from sense-deception,
from becoming, from history, from falsehood – history is
nothing but belief in the senses, belief in falsehood. Moral:
denial of all that believes in the senses, of all the rest of mankind: all of that is mere "people". Be a philosopher, be a
mummy, represent monotono-theism by a gravedigger-
mimicry! – And away, above all, with the *body*, that pitiable
idée fixe of the senses! infected with every error of logic there
is, refuted, impossible even, notwithstanding it is impudent
enough to behave as if it actually existed!' ...

* from the viewpoint of eternity.

2

I set apart with high reverence the name of *Heraclitus*. When the rest of the philosopher crowd rejected the evidence of the senses because these showed plurality and change, he rejected their evidence because they showed things as if they possessed duration and unity. Heraclitus too was unjust to the senses, which lie neither in the way the Eleatics* believe nor as he believed – they do not lie at all. It is what we *make* of their evidence that first introduces a lie into it, for example the lie of unity, the lie of materiality, of substance, of duration. . . . 'Reason' is the cause of our falsification of the evidence of the senses. In so far as the senses show becoming, passing away, change, they do not lie. . . . But Heraclitus will always be right in this, that being is an empty fiction. The 'apparent' world is the only one: the 'real' world has only been *lyingly added* . . .

3

– And what subtle instruments for observation we possess in our senses! This nose, for example, of which no philosopher has hitherto spoken with respect and gratitude, is nonetheless the most delicate tool we have at our command: it can detect minimal differences in movement which even the spectroscope cannot detect. We possess scientific knowledge today to precisely the extent that we have decided to *accept* the evidence of the senses – to the extent that we have learned to sharpen and arm them and to think them through to their conclusions. The rest is abortion and not-yet-science: which is to say metaphysics, theology, psychology, epistemology. *Or* science of formulae, sign-systems: such as logic and that applied logic, mathematics. In these reality does not appear at all, not even as a problem; just as little as does the question what value a system of conventional signs such as constitutes logic can possibly possess.† –

* The school of Parmenides of Elea (fifth century B.C.), who denied the logical possibility of change and motion and argued that the only logical possibility was unchanging being.

† A note on Nietzsche's estimation of logic will be found as Appendix B.

4

The *other* idiosyncrasy of philosophers is no less perilous: it consists in mistaking the last for the first. They put that which comes at the end – unfortunately! for it ought not to come at all! – the 'highest concepts', that is to say the most general, the emptiest concepts, the last fumes of evaporating reality, at the beginning *as* the beginning. It is again only the expression of their way of doing reverence: the higher must not be *allowed* to grow out of the lower, must not be *allowed* to have grown at all. . . . Moral: everything of the first rank must be *causa sui*.* Origin in something else counts as an objection, as casting a doubt on value. All supreme values are of the first rank, all the supreme concepts – that which is, the unconditioned, the good, the true, the perfect – all that cannot have become, *must* therefore be *causa sui*. But neither can these supreme concepts be incommensurate with one another, be incompatible with one another. . . . Thus they acquired their stupendous concept 'God'. . . . The last, thinnest, emptiest is placed as the first, as cause in itself, as *ens realissimum*.† . . . That mankind should have taken seriously the brainsick fancies of morbid cobweb-spinners! – And it has paid dearly for doing so! . . .

5

– Let us, in conclusion, set against this the very different way in which *we* (– I say 'we' out of politeness . . .) view the problem of error and appearance. Change, mutation, becoming in general were formerly taken as proof of appearance, as a sign of the presence of something which led us astray. Today, on the contrary, we see ourselves as it were entangled in error, *necessitated* to error, to precisely the extent that our prejudice in favour of reason compels us to posit unity, identity, duration, substance, cause, materiality, being; however sure we may be, on the basis of a strict reckoning, *that* error is to be found here. The situation is the same as with the motions of the sun: in that case error has our eyes, in the present case our *language*

* the cause of itself.   † the most real being.

as a perpetual advocate. Language belongs in its origin to the age of the most rudimentary form of psychology: we find ourselves in the midst of a rude fetishism when we call to mind the basic presuppositions of the metaphysics of language – which is to say, of *reason*. It is *this* which sees everywhere deed and doer; this which believes in will as cause in general; this which believes in the 'ego', in the ego as being, in the ego as substance, and which *projects* its belief in the ego-substance on to all things – only thus does it *create* the concept 'thing'. . . . Being is everywhere thought in, *foisted on*, as cause; it is only from the conception 'ego' that there follows, derivatively, the concept 'being'. . . . At the beginning stands the great fateful error that the will is something which *produces an effect* – that will is a *faculty*. . . . Today we know it is merely a word. . . . Very much later, in a world a thousand times more enlightened, the *security*, the subjective *certainty* with which the categories of reason* could be employed came all of a sudden into philosophers' heads: they concluded that these could not have originated in the empirical world – indeed, the entire empirical world was incompatible with them. *Where then do they originate?* – And in India as in Greece they committed the same blunder: 'We must once have dwelt in a higher world' – instead of *in a very much lower one*, which would have been the truth! – 'we must have been divine, *for* we possess reason!' . . . Nothing, in fact, has hitherto had a more direct power of persuasion than the error of being as it was formulated by, for example, the Eleatics: for every word, every sentence we utter speaks in its favour! – Even the opponents of the Eleatics were still subject to the seductive influence of their concept of being: Democritus, among others, when he invented his *atom*. . . . 'Reason' in language: oh what a deceitful old woman! I fear we are not getting rid of God because we still believe in grammar . . .†

---

* The context makes it clear that this Kantian-sounding term is not being employed in the sense of Kant's twelve *a priori* 'categories', but simply to mean the faculty of reasoning.

† For a note on Nietzsche's view of the relation between language and philosophy, see Appendix C.

6

It will be a matter for gratitude if I now compress so fundamental and new an insight into four theses: I shall thereby make it easier to understand, I shall thereby challenge contradiction.

First proposition. The grounds upon which 'this' world has been designated as apparent establish rather its reality – *another* kind of reality is absolutely undemonstrable.

Second proposition. The characteristics which have been assigned to the 'real being' of things are the characteristics of non-being, of *nothingness* – the 'real world' has been constructed out of the contradiction to the actual world: an apparent world indeed, in so far as it is no more than a *moral-optical* illusion.

Third proposition. To talk about 'another' world than this is quite pointless, provided that an instinct for slandering, disparaging and accusing life is not strong within us: in the latter case we *revenge* ourselves on life by means of the phantasmagoria of 'another', a 'better' life.

Fourth proposition. To divide the world into a 'real' and an 'apparent' world, whether in the manner of Christianity or in the manner of Kant (which is, after all, that of a *cunning* Christian –) is only a suggestion of *décadence* – a symptom of *declining* life. ... That the artist places a higher value on appearance than on reality constitutes no objection to this proposition. For 'appearance' here signifies reality *once more*, only selected, strengthened, corrected. ... The tragic artist is *not* a pessimist – it is precisely he who *affirms* all that is questionable and terrible in existence, he is *Dionysian** ...

* For an explanation of what the word 'Dionysian' means here and in Nietzsche's work in general, see 'Expeditions of an Untimely Man' 49 and Appendix H.

How the 'Real World' at last Became a Myth

HISTORY OF AN ERROR

1. The real world, attainable to the wise, the pious, the virtuous man – he dwells in it, *he is it*.

> (Oldest form of the idea, relatively sensible, simple, convincing. Transcription of the proposition 'I, Plato, *am* the truth.')*

2. The real world, unattainable for the moment, but promised to the wise, the pious, the virtuous man ('to the sinner who repents').

> (Progress of the idea: it grows more refined, more enticing, more incomprehensible – *it becomes a woman*, it becomes Christian . . .)

3. The real world, unattainable, undemonstrable, cannot be promised, but even when merely thought of a consolation, a duty, an imperative.

> (Fundamentally the same old sun, but shining through mist and scepticism; the idea grown sublime, pale, northerly, Königsbergian.)†

4. The real world – unattainable? Unattained, at any rate. And if unattained also *unknown*. Consequently also no consolation, no redemption, no duty: how could we have a duty towards something unknown?

> (The grey of dawn. First yawnings of reason. Cockcrow of positivism.)‡

5. The 'real world' – an idea no longer of any use, not even a duty any longer – an idea grown useless, superfluous, *consequently* a refuted idea: let us abolish it!

> (Broad daylight; breakfast; return of cheerfulness and

---

* the truth = *Wahrheit*, corresponding to *wahre Welt* = real world.

† i.e. Kantian, from the northerly German city in which Kant was born and in which he lived and died.

‡ Here meaning empiricism, philosophy founded on observation and experiment.

bon sens; Plato blushes for shame; all free spirits run riot.)

6. We have abolished the real world: what world is left? the apparent world perhaps? . . . But no! *with the real world we have also abolished the apparent world!*

(Mid-day; moment of the shortest shadow; end of the longest error; zenith of mankind; INCIPIT ZARA-THUSTRA.)*

* Here begins Zarathustra. For a note on Nietzsche's attitude towards metaphysics, see Appendix D.

Morality as Anti-Nature

I

THERE is a time with all passions when they are merely
fatalities, when they drag their victim down with the weight of
their folly – and a later, very much later time when they are
wedded with the spirit, when they are 'spiritualized'. Formerly one made war on passion itself on account of the folly
inherent in it: one conspired for its extermination – all the old
moral monsters are unanimous that '*il faut tuer les passions*'.*
The most famous formula for doing this is contained in the
New Testament, in the Sermon on the Mount, where, by the
way, things are not at all regarded from a *lofty* standpoint.
There, for example, it is said, with reference to sexuality, 'if
thy eye offend thee, pluck it out': fortunately no Christian
follows this prescription. To *exterminate* the passions and
desires merely in order to do away with their folly and its
unpleasant consequences – this itself seems to us today merely
an acute form of folly. We no longer admire dentists who *pull
out* the teeth to stop them hurting. . . . On the other hand, it is
only fair to admit that on the soil out of which Christianity
grew the concept '*spiritualization* of passion' could not possibly
be conceived. For the primitive Church, as is well known,
fought *against* the 'intelligent' in favour of the 'poor in
spirit': how could one expect from it an intelligent war
against passion? – The Church combats the passions with
excision in every sense of the word: its practice, its 'cure' is
castration. It never asks: 'How can one spiritualize, beautify,
deify a desire?' – it has at all times laid the emphasis of its
discipline on extirpation (of sensuality, of pride, of lust for
power, of avarice, of revengefulness). – But to attack the
passions at their roots means to attack life at its roots: the
practice of the Church is *hostile to life* . . .

* The passions must be killed.

42

2

The same expedient – castration, extirpation – is instinctively selected in a struggle against a desire by those who are too weak-willed, too degenerate to impose moderation upon it: by those natures which need La Trappe,* to speak metaphorically (and not metaphorically –), some sort of definitive declaration of hostility, a *chasm* between themselves and a passion. It is only the degenerate who cannot do without radical expedients; weakness of will, more precisely the inability *not* to react to a stimulus, is itself merely another form of degeneration. Radical hostility, mortal hostility towards sensuality is always a thought-provoking symptom: it justifies making certain conjectures as to the general condition of one who is excessive in this respect. – That hostility, that hatred reaches its height, moreover, only when such natures are no longer sufficiently sound even for the radical cure, for the renunciation of their 'devil'. Survey the entire history of priests and philosophers, and that of artists as well: the most virulent utterances against the senses have *not* come from the impotent, *nor* from ascetics, but from those who found it impossible to be ascetics, from those who stood in need of being ascetics ...

3

The spiritualization of sensuality is called *love*: it is a great triumph over Christianity. A further triumph is our spiritualization of *enmity*. It consists in profoundly grasping the value of having enemies: in brief, in acting and thinking in the reverse of the way in which one formerly acted and thought. The Church has at all times desired the destruction of its enemies: we, we immoralists and anti-Christians, see that it is to our advantage that the Church exist. ... In politics, too, enmity has become much more spiritual – much more prudent, much more thoughtful, much more *forbearing*. Almost every party grasps that it is in the interest of its own self-preserva-

* The abbey at Soligny from which the Trappist order – characterized by the severity of its discipline – takes it name.

tion that the opposing party should not decay in strength; the same is true of grand politics. A new creation in particular, the new *Reich* for instance, has more need of enemies than friends: only in opposition does it feel itself necessary, only in opposition does it *become* necessary. . . . We adopt the same attitude towards the 'enemy within': there too we have spiritualized enmity, there too we have grasped its *value*. One is *fruitful* only at the cost of being rich in contradictions; one remains *young* only on condition the soul does not relax, does not long for peace. . . . Nothing has grown more alien to us than that desideratum of former times 'peace of soul', the *Christian* desideratum; nothing arouses less envy in us than the moral cow and the fat contentment of the good conscience. . . . One has renounced *grand* life when one renounces war. . . . In many cases, to be sure, 'peace of soul' is merely a misunderstanding – something *else* that simply does not know how to give itself a more honest name. Here, briefly and without prejudice, are a few of them. 'Peace of soul' can, for example, be the gentle radiation of a rich animality into the moral (or religious) domain. Or the beginning of weariness, the first of the shadows which evening, every sort of evening, casts. Or a sign that the air is damp, that south winds are on the way. Or unconscious gratitude for a good digestion (sometimes called 'philanthropy'). Or the quiescence of the convalescent for whom all things have a new taste and who waits. . . . Or the condition which succeeds a vigorous gratification of our ruling passion, the pleasant feeling of a rare satiety. Or the decrepitude of our will, our desires, our vices. Or laziness persuaded by vanity to deck itself out as morality. Or the appearance of a certainty, even a dreadful certainty, after the protracted tension and torture of uncertainty. Or the expression of ripeness and mastery in the midst of action, creation, endeavour, volition, a quiet breathing, 'freedom of will' *attained*. . . . *Twilight of the Idols:* who knows? perhaps that too is only a kind of 'peace of soul' . . .

4

– I formulate a principle. All naturalism in morality, that is all *healthy* morality, is dominated by an instinct of life – some commandment of life is fulfilled through a certain canon of 'shall' and 'shall not', some hindrance and hostile element on life's road is thereby removed. *Anti-natural* morality, that is virtually every morality that has hitherto been taught, reverenced and preached, turns on the contrary precisely *against* the instincts of life – it is a now secret, now loud and impudent *condemnation* of these instincts. By saying 'God sees into the heart' it denies the deepest and the highest desires of life and takes God for the *enemy of life*. . . . The saint in whom God takes pleasure is the ideal castrate. . . . Life is at an end where the 'kingdom of God' *begins* . . .

5

If one has grasped the blasphemousness of such a rebellion against life as has, in Christian morality, become virtually sacrosanct, one has fortunately therewith grasped something else as well: the uselessness, illusoriness, absurdity, *falsity* of such a rebellion. For a condemnation of life by the living is after all no more than the symptom of a certain kind of life: the question whether the condemnation is just or unjust has not been raised at all. One would have to be situated *outside* life, and on the other hand to know it as thoroughly as any, as many, as all who have experienced it, to be permitted to touch on the problem of the *value* of life at all: sufficient reason for understanding that this problem is for us an inaccessible problem. When we speak of values we do so under the inspiration and from the perspective of life: life itself evaluates through us *when* we establish values. . . . From this it follows that even that *anti-nature of a morality* which conceives God as the contrary concept to and condemnation of life is only a value judgement on the part of life – of *what* life? of *what* kind of life? – But I have already given the answer: of declining, debilitated, weary, condemned life. Morality as it has been understood hitherto – as it was ultimately formulated by

Schopenhauer as 'denial of the will to life' – is the *instinct of décadence* itself, which makes out of itself an imperative: it says: 'Perish!' – it is the judgement of the judged . . .

6

Let us consider finally what naïvety it is to say 'man *ought* to be thus and thus!' Reality shows us an enchanting wealth of types, the luxuriance of a prodigal play and change of forms: and does some pitiful journeyman moralist say at the sight of it: 'No! man ought to be *different*'? . . . He even knows *how* man ought to be, this bigoted wretch; he paints himself on the wall and says '*ecce homo*'!* . . . But even when the moralist merely turns to the individual and says to him: '*You* ought to be thus and thus' he does not cease to make himself ridiculous. The individual is, in his future and in his past, a piece of fate, one law more, one necessity more for everything that is and everything that will be. To say to him 'change yourself' means to demand that everything should change, even in the past. . . . And there have indeed been consistent moralists who wanted man to be different, namely virtuous, who wanted him in their own likeness, namely that of a bigot: to that end they *denied* the world! No mean madness! No modest presumption! . . . In so far as morality *condemns* as morality and *not* with regard to the aims and objects of life, it is a specific error with which one should show no sympathy, an *idiosyncrasy of the degenerate* which has caused an unspeakable amount of harm! . . . We others, we immoralists, have on the contrary opened wide our hearts to every kind of understanding, comprehension, *approval*. We do not readily deny, we seek our honour in *affirming*. We have come more and more to appreciate that economy which needs and knows how to use all that which the holy lunacy of the priest, the *diseased* reason of the priest rejects; that economy in the law of life which derives advantage even from the repellent species of the bigot, the priest, the virtuous man – *what* advantage? – But we ourselves, we immoralists, are the answer to that . . .

* Behold the man!

46

The Four Great Errors

1

The error of mistaking cause for consequence. – There is no more dangerous error than that of *mistaking the consequence for the cause:* I call it reason's intrinsic form of corruption. Nonetheless, this error is among the most ancient and most recent habits of mankind: it is even sanctified among us, it bears the names 'religion' and 'morality'. *Every* proposition formulated by religion and morality contains it; priests and moral legislators are the authors of this corruption of reason. – I adduce an example. Everyone knows the book of the celebrated Cornaro in which he recommends his meagre diet as a recipe for a long and happy life – a virtuous one, too. Few books have been so widely read; even now many thousands of copies are printed in England every year. I do not doubt that hardly any book (the Bible rightly excepted) has done so much harm, has shortened so many lives, as this curiosity, which was so well meant. The reason: mistaking the consequence for the cause. The worthy Italian saw in his diet the *cause* of his long life: while the prerequisite of long life, an extraordinarily slow metabolism, a small consumption, was the cause of his meagre diet. He was not free to eat much *or* little as he chose, his frugality was *not* an act of 'free will': he became ill when he ate more. But if one is not a bony fellow of this sort one does not merely do well, one positively needs to eat *properly*. A scholar of *our* day, with his rapid consumption of nervous energy, would kill himself with Cornaro's regimen. *Credo experto.* –

2

The most general formula at the basis of every religion and morality is: 'Do this and this, refrain from this and this – and you will be happy! Otherwise. . . .' Every morality, every religion *is* this imperative – I call it the great original sin of

47

reason, *immortal unreason*. In my mouth this formula is converted into its reverse – *first* example of my 'revaluation of all values': a well-constituted human being, a 'happy one', *must* perform certain actions and instinctively shrinks from other actions, he transports the order of which he is the physiological representative into his relations with other human beings and with things. In a formula: his virtue is the *consequence* of his happiness. . . . Long life, a plentiful posterity is *not* the reward of virtue, virtue itself is rather just that slowing down of the metabolism which also has, among other things, a long life, a plentiful posterity, in short *Cornarism*, as its outcome. – The Church and morality say: 'A race, a people perishes through vice and luxury'. My *restored* reason says: when a people is perishing, degenerating physiologically, vice and luxury (that is to say the necessity for stronger and stronger and more and more frequent stimulants, such as every exhausted nature is acquainted with) *follow* therefrom. A young man grows prematurely pale and faded. His friends say: this and that illness is to blame. I say: *that* he became ill, *that* he failed to resist the illness, was already the consequence of an impoverished life, an hereditary exhaustion. The newspaper reader says: this party will ruin itself if it makes errors like this. My *higher* politics says: a party which makes errors like this is already finished – it is no longer secure in its instincts. Every error, of whatever kind, is a consequence of degeneration of instinct, disgregation of will: one has thereby virtually defined the *bad*. Everything *good* is instinct – and consequently easy, necessary, free. Effort is an objection, the *god* is typically distinguished from the hero (in my language: *light* feet are the first attribute of divinity).

3

The error of a false causality. – We have always believed we know what a cause is: but whence did we derive our knowledge, more precisely our belief we possessed this knowledge? From the realm of the celebrated 'inner facts', none of which has up till now been shown to be factual. We believed ourselves to be causal agents in the act of willing; we at least thought we were there *catching causality in the act*. It was likewise never doubted that all the *antecedentia* of an action, its causes, were to be sought in the consciousness and could be discovered there if one sought them – as 'motives': for otherwise one would not have been *free* to perform it, *responsible* for it. Finally, who would have disputed that a thought is caused? that the ego causes the thought? ... Of these three 'inner facts' through which causality seemed to be guaranteed the first and most convincing was that of *will as cause*; the conception of a consciousness ('mind') as cause and later still that of the ego (the 'subject') as cause are merely after-products after causality had, on the basis of will, been firmly established as a given fact, as *empiricism*. ... Meanwhile we have thought better. Today we do not believe a word of it. The 'inner world' is full of phantoms and false lights: the will is one of them. The will no longer moves anything, consequently no longer explains anything – it merely accompanies events, it can also be absent. The so-called 'motive': another error. Merely a surface phenomenon of consciousness, an accompaniment to an act, which conceals rather than exposes the *antecedentia* of the act. And as for the ego! It has become a fable, a fiction, a play on words: it has totally ceased to think, to feel and to will! ... What follows from this? There are no spiritual causes at all! The whole of the alleged empiricism which affirmed them has gone to the devil! *That* is what follows! – And we had made a nice misuse of that 'empiricism', we had *created* the world on the basis of it as a world of causes, as a world of will, as a world of spirit. The oldest and longest-lived psychology was at work here – indeed it has done nothing else: every event was to it an action, every action the effect of a will, the world became for it a multiplicity of agents, an agent ('subject') foisted itself upon every event. Man projected his three 'inner facts', that in which he believed more firmly than in anything else, will, spirit, ego, outside himself – he derived the concept 'being' only from the concept 'ego', he posited 'things' as possessing being according to his own image, according to his concept of the ego as cause. No wonder he later always discovered in things only *that which he had put into them!* – The thing itself, to say it again, the concept 'thing' is merely a reflection of the belief in the ego as cause. . . . And even your atom, *messieurs* mechanists and physicists, how much error, how much rudimentary psychology, still remains in your atom! – To say nothing of the 'thing in itself',* that *horrendum pudendum*† of the metaphysicians! The error of spirit as cause mistaken for reality! And made the measure of reality! And called *God*! –

4

The error of imaginary causes. – To start from the dream: on to a certain sensation, the result for example of a distant cannon-shot, a cause is subsequently foisted (often a whole little novel in which precisely the dreamer is the chief character). The sensation, meanwhile, continues to persist, as a kind of resonance: it waits, as it were, until the cause-creating drive permits it to step into the foreground – now no longer as a chance occurrence but as 'meaning'. The cannon-shot enters in a *causal* way, in an apparent inversion of time. That which comes later, the motivation, is experienced first, often with a hundred details which pass like lightning, the shot *follows*. . . . What has happened? The ideas *engendered* by a certain condition have been misunderstood as the cause of that condition. – We do just the same thing, in fact, when we are awake. Most of our general feelings – every sort of restraint, pressure, tension, explosion in the play and counter-play of our organs, likewise and especially the condition of the *nervus sympathicus* – excite our cause-creating drive: we want to have a *reason* for feeling *as we do* – for feeling well or for feeling ill. It never suffices us simply to establish the mere fact *that* we feel as we do: we acknowledge this fact – become *conscious* of it – only

---

* In Kant's philosophy the causes of sensations are called 'things in themselves'. The thing in itself is unknowable: the sensations we actually experience are produced by the operation of our subjective mental apparatus.

† ugly shameful part.

when we have furnished it with a motivation of some kind. –
The memory, which in such a case becomes active without
our being aware of it, calls up earlier states of a similar kind
and the causal interpretations which have grown out of them –
not their causality. To be sure, the belief that these ideas, the
accompanying occurrences in the consciousness, were causes is
also brought up by the memory. Thus there arises an *habitua-
tion* to a certain causal interpretation which in truth obstructs
and even prohibits an *investigation* of the cause.

5

Psychological explanation. – To trace something unknown back
to something known is alleviating, soothing, gratifying and
gives moreover a feeling of power. Danger, disquiet, anxiety
attend the unknown – the first instinct is to *eliminate* these
distressing states. First principle: any explanation is better
than none. Because it is at bottom only a question of wanting
to get rid of oppressive ideas, one is not exactly particular
about what means one uses to get rid of them: the first idea
which explains that the unknown is in fact the known does so
much good that one 'holds it for true'. Proof by *pleasure*
('by potency') as criterion of truth. – The cause-creating
drive is thus conditioned and excited by the feeling of fear.
The question 'why?' should furnish, if at all possible, not so
much the cause for its own sake as a *certain kind of cause* – a
soothing, liberating, alleviating cause. That something already
known, experienced, inscribed in the memory is posited as
cause is the first consequence of this need. The new, the unexperienced, the strange is excluded from being cause. – Thus
there is sought not only some kind of explanation as cause, but
a *selected* and *preferred* kind of explanation, the kind by means of
which the feeling of the strange, new, unexperienced is most
speedily and most frequently abolished – the *most common*
explanations. – Consequence: a particular kind of cause-
ascription comes to preponderate more and more, becomes
concentrated into a system and finally comes to *dominate* over
the rest, that is to say simply to exclude *other* causes and

explanations. – The banker thinks at once of 'business', the Christian of 'sin', the girl of her love.

6

The entire realm of morality and religion falls under this concept of imaginary causes. – 'Explanation' of *unpleasant* general feelings. They arise from beings hostile to us (evil spirits: most celebrated case – hysterics misunderstood as witches). They arise from actions we cannot approve of (the feeling of 'sin', of 'culpability' foisted upon a physiological discomfort – one always finds reasons for being discontented with oneself). They arise as punishments, as payment for something we should not have done, should not have *been* (generalized in an impudent form by Schopenhauer into a proposition in which morality appears for what it is, the actual poisoner and calumniator of life: 'Every great pain, whether physical or mental, declares what it is we deserve; for it could not have come upon us if we had not deserved it.' *World as Will and Idea* II 666). They arise as the consequences of rash actions which have turned out badly (– the emotions, the senses assigned as 'cause', as 'to blame'; physiological states of distress construed, with the aid of *other* states of distress, as 'deserved'). – 'Explanation' of *pleasant* general feelings. They arise from trust in God. They arise from the consciousness of good actions (the so-called 'good conscience', a physiological condition sometimes so like a sound digestion as to be mistaken for it). They arise from the successful outcome of undertakings (– naïve fallacy: the successful outcome of an undertaking certainly does not produce any pleasant general feelings in a hypochondriac or a Pascal). They arise from faith, hope and charity – the Christian virtues. – In reality all these supposed explanations are *consequential* states and as it were translations of pleasurable and unpleasurable feelings into a false dialect: one is in a state in which one can experience hope *because* the physiological basic feeling is once more strong and ample; one trusts in God *because* the feeling of plenitude and strength makes one calm. – Morality and religion fall entirely under the *psychology of error*: in every single case cause is mistaken for effect; or the effect of what is *believed* true is mistaken for the truth; or a state of consciousness is mistaken for the causation of this state.

7

The error of free will. – We no longer have any sympathy today with the concept of 'free will': we know only too well what it is – the most infamous of all the arts of the theologian for making mankind 'accountable' in his sense of the word, that is to say for *making mankind dependent on him*. . . . I give here only the psychology of making men accountable. – Everywhere accountability is sought, it is usually the instinct for *punishing and judging* which seeks it. One has deprived becoming of its innocence if being in this or that state is traced back to will, to intentions, to accountable acts: the doctrine of will has been invented essentially for the purpose of punishment, that is of *finding guilty*. The whole of the old-style psychology, the psychology of will, has as its precondition the desire of its authors, the priests at the head of the ancient communities, to create for themselves a *right* to ordain punishments – or their desire to create for God a right to do so. . . . Men were thought of as 'free' so that they could become *guilty*: consequently, every action *had* to be thought of as willed, the origin of every action as lying in the consciousness (– whereby the most *fundamental* falsification *in psychologicis* was made into the very principle of psychology). . . . Today, when we have started to move in the *reverse* direction, when we immoralists especially are trying with all our might to remove the concept of guilt and the concept of punishment from the world and to purge psychology, history, nature, the social institutions and sanctions of them, there is in our eyes no more radical opposition than that of the theologians, who continue to infect the innocence of becoming with 'punishment' and 'guilt' by means of the concept of the 'moral world-order'. Christianity is a hangman's metaphysics . . .

8

What alone can *our* teaching be? – That no one *gives* a human being his qualities: not God, not society, not his parents or ancestors, not *he himself* (– the nonsensical idea here last rejected was propounded, as 'intelligible freedom', by Kant, and perhaps also by Plato before him). *No one* is accountable for existing at all, or for being constituted as he is, or for living in the circumstances and surroundings in which he lives. The fatality of his nature cannot be disentangled from the fatality of all that which has been and will be. He is *not* the result of a special design, a will, a purpose; he is *not* the subject of an attempt to attain to an 'ideal of man' or an 'ideal of happiness' or an 'ideal of morality' – it is absurd to want to *hand over* his nature to some purpose or other. *We* invented the concept 'purpose': in reality purpose is *lacking*. . . . One is necessary, one is a piece of fate, one belongs to the whole, one *is* in the whole – there exists nothing which could judge, measure, compare, condemn our being, for that would be to judge, measure, compare, condemn the whole. . . . *But nothing exists apart from the whole!* – That no one is any longer made accountable, that the kind of being manifested cannot be traced back to a *causa prima*,* that the world is a unity neither as sensorium nor as 'spirit', *this alone is the great liberation* – thus alone is the *innocence* of becoming restored. . . . The concept 'God' has hitherto been the greatest *objection* to existence. . . . We deny God; in denying God, we deny accountability: only by doing *that* do we redeem the world. – †

* first cause.
† A note on Nietzsche's epistemology will be found as Appendix E.

The 'Improvers' of Mankind

I

One knows my demand of philosophers that they place themselves *beyond* good and evil – that they have the illusion of
moral judgement *beneath* them. This demand follows from an
insight first formulated by me: *that there are no moral facts
whatever*. Moral judgement has this in common with religious
judgement that it believes in realities which do not exist.
Morality is only an interpretation of certain phenomena, more
precisely a *mis*interpretation. Moral judgement belongs, as
does religious judgement, to a level of ignorance at which
even the concept of the real, the distinction between the real
and the imaginary, is lacking: so that at such a level 'truth'
denotes nothing but things which we today call 'imaginings'.
To this extent moral judgement is never to be taken literally:
as such it never contains anything but nonsense. But as *seme-
iotics* it remains of incalculable value: it reveals, to the in-
formed man at least, the most precious realities of cultures and
inner worlds which did not *know* enough to 'understand'
themselves. Morality is merely sign-language, merely sympto-
matology: one must already know *what* it is about to derive
profit from it.

2

A first example, merely as an introduction. In all ages one has
wanted to 'improve' men: this above all is what morality has
meant. But one word can conceal the most divergent tenden-
cies. Both the *taming* of the beast man and the *breeding* of a certain species of man has been called 'improvement': only these
zoological *termini* express realities – realities, to be sure, of
which the typical 'improver', the priest, knows nothing –
wants to know nothing. . . . To call the taming of an animal its
'improvement' is in our ears almost a joke. Whoever knows

what goes on in menageries is doubtful whether the beasts in them are 'improved'. They are weakened, they are made less harmful, they become *sickly* beasts through the depressive emotion of fear, through pain, through injuries, through hunger. – It is no different with the tamed human being whom the priest has 'improved'. In the early Middle Ages, when the Church was in fact above all a menagerie, one everywhere hunted down the fairest specimens of the 'blond beast'* – one 'improved', for example, the noble Teutons. But what did such a Teuton afterwards look like when he had been 'improved' and led into a monastery? Like a caricature of a human being, like an abortion: he had become a 'sinner', he was in a cage, one had imprisoned him behind nothing but sheer terrifying concepts. . . . There he lay now, sick, miserable, filled with ill-will towards himself; full of hatred for the impulses towards life, full of suspicion of all that was still strong and happy. In short, a 'Christian'. . . . In physiological terms: in the struggle with the beast, making it sick *can* be the only means of making it weak. This the Church understood: it *corrupted* the human being, it weakened him – but it claimed to have 'improved' him. . .

3

Let us take the other aspect of so-called morality, the *breeding* of a definite race and species. The most grandiose example of this is provided by Indian morality, sanctioned, as the 'Law of Manu', into religion. Here the proposed task is to breed no fewer than four races simultaneously: a priestly, a warrior, and a trading and farming race, and finally a menial race, the

* Nietzsche introduced this term in *Towards a Genealogy of Morals* I 11: it means man considered as an animal, and the first use of the term is immediately followed by a reference to 'the Roman, Arab, Teutonic, Japanese nobility, the Homeric heroes, the Scandinavian Vikings' and to the Athenians of the age of Pericles as examples of men 'the animal' in whom 'has to get out again, has to go back to the wilderness.' The uses of 'blond beast' are not fully intelligible apart from Nietzsche's psychology, for a note on which see Appendix F.

Sudras. Here we are manifestly no longer among animal-tamers: a species of human being a hundred times more gentle and rational is presupposed even to conceive the plan of such a breeding. One draws a breath of relief when coming out of the Christian sick-house and dungeon atmosphere into this healthier, higher, *wider* world. How paltry the 'New Testament' is compared with Manu, how ill it smells! – But this organization too needed to be *dreadful* – this time in struggle not with the beast but with *its* antithesis, with the non-bred human being, the hotchpotch human being, the Chandala.* And again it had no means of making him weak and harmless other than making him *sick* – it was the struggle with the 'great majority'. Perhaps there is nothing which outrages our feelings more than *these* protective measures of Indian morality. The third edict, for example (*Avadana-Shastra* I), that 'concerning unclean vegetables', ordains that the only nourishment permitted the Chandala shall be garlic and onions, in view of the fact that holy scripture forbids one to give them corn or seed-bearing fruits or *water* or fire. The same edict lays it down that the water they need must not be taken from rivers or springs or pools, but only from the entrances to swamps and holes made by the feet of animals. They are likewise forbidden to wash their clothes or to *wash themselves*, since the water allowed them as an act of charity must be used only for quenching the thirst. Finally, the Sudra women are forbidden to assist the Chandala women in childbirth, and the latter are likewise forbidden to *assist one another*. ... – The harvest of such hygienic regulations did not fail to appear: murderous epidemics, hideous venereal diseases and, as a consequence, 'the law of the knife' once more, ordaining circumcision for the male and removal of the *labia minora* for the female children. – Manu himself says: 'The Chandala are the fruit of adultery, incest and crime' (– this being the *necessary* consequence of the concept 'breeding'). 'They shall have for clothing only rags from corpses, for utensils broken pots, for ornaments old iron, for worship only evil spirits; they shall wander from place to place without rest. They are

* The 'untouchables' excluded from the caste system.

forbidden to write from left to right and to use the right hand for writing: the employment of the right hand and of the left-to-right motion is reserved for the *virtuous*, for people of *race*.' –

4

These regulations are instructive enough: in them we find for once *Aryan* humanity, quite pure, quite primordial – we learn that the concept 'pure blood' is the opposite of a harmless concept. It becomes clear, on the other hand, in *which* people the hatred, the Chandala hatred for this 'humanity' has been immortalized, where it has become religion, where it has become *genius*. ... From this point of view, the Gospels are documents of the first rank; the Book of Enoch even more so. – Christianity, growing from Jewish roots and comprehensible only as a product of this soil,* represents the *reaction* against that morality of breeding, of race, of privilege – it is the *anti-Aryan* religion *par excellence*: Christianity the revaluation of all Aryan values, the victory of Chandala values, the evangel preached to the poor and lowly, the collective rebellion of everything downtrodden, wretched, ill-constituted, under-privileged against the 'race' – undying Chandala revenge as the *religion of love* ...

5

The morality of *breeding* and the morality of *taming* are, in the means they employ to attain their ends, entirely worthy of one another: we may set down as our chief proposition that to *make* morality one must have the unconditional will to the contrary. This is the great, the *uncanny* problem which I have pursued furthest: the psychology of the 'improvers' of mankind. A small and really rather modest fact, that of so-called *pia fraus*,† gave me my first access to this problem: *pia fraus*, the heritage of all philosophers and priests who have 'improved' mankind. Neither Manu nor Plato, neither Confucius

* This is one of the major themes of *The Anti-Christ*.
† pious fraud.

nor the Jewish and Christian teachers, ever doubted their *right* to tell lies. Nor did they doubt their possession of *other rights*. . . . Expressed in a formula one might say: *every* means hitherto employed with the intention of making mankind moral has been thoroughly *immoral*. – *

* For a note on Nietzsche's study of morality, see Appendix G.

What the Germans Lack

I

Among Germans today it is not enough to possess spirit: one must also possess the *presumption* to possess it ...

Perhaps I know the Germans, perhaps I might even venture to address a few words to them. The new Germany represents a great quantity of inherited and inculcated ability, so that it may for a time be allowed even a lavish expenditure of its accumulated store of energy. It is *not* a high culture that has here gained ascendancy, even less a fastidious taste, a noble 'beauty' of the instincts, but more manly virtues than any other country of Europe can exhibit. A good deal of courage and respect for oneself, a good deal of self-confidence in social dealings and in the performance of reciprocal duties, a good deal of industriousness, a good deal of endurance – and an inherited moderation which requires the goad rather than the brake. I also add that here people can still obey without being humiliated by obeying. . . . And no one despises his adversary ...

You will see I want to be just to the Germans: I would not like to be untrue to myself in this – so I must also tell them what I object to. Coming to power is a costly business: power *makes stupid.* . . . The Germans – once they were called the nation of thinkers: do they still think at all? Nowadays the Germans are bored with intellect, the Germans mistrust intellect, politics devours all seriousness for really intellectual things – *Deutschland, Deutschland über alles* was, I fear, the end of German philosophy. . . . 'Are there any German philosophers? are there any German poets? are there any *good* German books?' – people ask me abroad. I blush; but with the courage which is mine even in desperate cases I answer: 'Yes, *Bismarck*!' – Dare I go so far as to confess which books are read nowadays? . . . Confounded instinct of mediocrity! –

2

– Who has not pondered sadly over what the German spirit *could* be! But this nation has deliberately made itself stupid, for practically a thousand years: nowhere else are the two great European narcotics, alcohol and Christianity, so viciously abused. Lately even a third has been added, one which is capable by itself of completely obstructing all delicate and audacious flexibility of spirit: music, our constipated, constipating German music. – How much dreary heaviness, lameness, dampness, sloppiness, how much *beer* there is in the German intellect! How can it possibly happen that young men who dedicate their existence to the most spiritual goals lack all sense of the first instinct of spirituality, *the spirit's instinct for self-preservation* – and drink beer? ... The alcoholism of scholarly youth perhaps does not constitute a question-mark in regard to their erudition – one can be even a great scholar without possessing any spirit at all – but from any other point of view it remains a problem. – Where does one not find that bland degeneration which beer produces in the spirit! Once, in a case that has become almost famous, I laid my finger on such an instance of degeneration – the degeneration of our first German freethinker, the *shrewd* David Strauss, into the author of an ale-house gospel and a 'new faith'.... It was no vain vow he made in verse to the 'gracious brunette'* – fidelity unto death ...

3

– I have said of the German spirit that it is growing coarser, that it is growing shallow. Is that sufficient? – Fundamentally, it is something quite different which appals me: how German seriousness, German profundity, German *passion* in spiritual things is more and more on the decline. It is the pathos and not merely the intellectual aspect which has altered. – I come in contact now and then with German universities: what an atmosphere prevails among its scholars, what a barren spirituality, grown how contented and lukewarm! It would be

* beer.

a profound misunderstanding to adduce German science as an objection here, as well as being proof one had not read a word I have written. For seventeen years I have not wearied of exposing the *despiritualizing* influence of our contemporary scientific pursuits. The harsh Helot condition to which the tremendous extent of science has condemned every single person today is one of the main reasons why education *and educators* appropriate to fuller, richer, *deeper* natures are no longer forthcoming. Our culture suffers from nothing *more* than it suffers from the superabundance of presumptuous journeymen and fragments of humanity; our universities are, *against* their will, the actual forcing-houses for this kind of spiritual instinct-atrophy. And all Europe already has an idea of this – grand politics deceives no one. . . . Germany counts more and more as Europe's *flatland*. – I am still *looking* for a German with whom *I* could be serious after my fashion – how much more for one with whom I might be cheerful! – *Twilight of the Idols*: ah, who today could grasp *from how profound a seriousness* a hermit is here relaxing! – The most incomprehensible thing about us is our cheerfulness . . .

4

If one makes a reckoning, it is obvious not only that German culture is declining, the sufficient reason* for it is obvious too. After all, no one can spend more than he has – that is true of individuals, it is also true of nations. If one spends oneself on power, grand politics, economic affairs, world commerce, parliamentary institutions, military interests – if one expends in *this* direction the quantum of reason, seriousness, will, self-overcoming that one is, then there will be a shortage in the other direction. Culture and the state – one should not deceive oneself over this – are antagonists: the 'cultural state' is merely a modern idea. The one lives off the other, the one

---

* A philosophical term meaning an explanation of something adequate to explaining it fully. Schopenhauer's doctoral thesis was *On the Fourfold Root of the Principle of Sufficient Reason*, and Nietzsche sometimes (as here) uses the term in a humorously inappropriate context.

thrives at the expense of the other. All great cultural epochs are epochs of political decline: that which is great in the cultural sense has been unpolitical, even *anti-political*. . . . Goethe's heart opened up at the phenomenon Napoleon – it *closed* up to the 'Wars of Liberation'. . . . The moment Germany rises as a great power, France gains a new importance as a *cultural power*. A great deal of current spiritual seriousness and *passion* has already emigrated to Paris; the question of pessimism, for instance, the Wagner question, virtually every psychological and artistic question, is speculated on with incomparably more subtlety and thoroughness there than in Germany – the Germans are even *incapable* of this kind of seriousness. – In the history of European culture the rise of the 'Reich' signifies one thing above all: a *displacement of the centre of gravity*. The fact is known everywhere: in the main thing – and that is still culture – the Germans no longer come into consideration. The question is asked: haven't you so much as one spirit who *means something* to Europe? in the way your Goethe, your Hegel, your Heinrich Heine, your Schopenhauer meant something? That there is no longer a single German philosopher – there is no end of astonishment at that. –

5

The essential thing has gone out of the entire system of higher education in Germany: the *end*, as well as the *means* to the end. That education, *culture*, itself is the end – and *not* 'the Reich' – that *educators* are required for the attainment of this end – and *not* grammar-school teachers and university scholars – that too has been forgotten. . . . There is a need for educators *who are themselves educated*; superior, noble spirits, who prove themselves every moment by what they say and by what they do not say: cultures grown ripe and *sweet* – and *not* the learned boors which grammar school and university offer youth today as 'higher nurses'. Educators, the *first* prerequisite of education, are *lacking* (except for the exceptions of exceptions): *hence* the decline of German culture. – One of those rarest of exceptions is my honoured friend Jacob

Burckhardt of Basel: it is to him above all that Basel owes its pre-eminence in the humanities. – What the 'higher schools' of Germany in fact achieve is a brutal breaking-in with the aim of making, in the least possible time, numberless young men fit to be utilized, *utilized to the full and used up*, in the state service. 'Higher education' and *numberless* – that is a contradiction to start with. All higher education belongs to the exceptions alone: one must be privileged to have a right to so high a privilege. Great and fine things can never be common property: *pulchrum est paucorum hominum*.* – What is the *cause* of the decline of German culture? That 'higher education' is no longer a privilege – the democratism of 'culture' made 'universal' and *common*. .... Not to overlook the fact that military privileges absolutely compel *too great attendance* at higher schools, which means their ruin. – No one is any longer free in present-day Germany to give his children a noble education: our 'higher' schools are one and all adjusted – as regards their teachers, their curricula and their instructional aims – to the most dubious mediocrity. And there reigns everywhere an indecent haste, as if something has been neglected if the young man of twenty-three is not yet 'finished and ready', does not yet know the answer to the 'chief question': *which* calling? – A higher kind of human being, excuse me for saying, doesn't think much of 'callings', the reason being he knows himself called. .... He takes his time, he has plenty of time, he gives no thought whatsoever to being 'finished and ready' – at the age of thirty one is, as regards high culture, a beginner, a child. – Our overcrowded grammar schools, our overloaded, stupified grammar-school teachers, are a scandal: one may perhaps have *motives* for defending this state of things, as the professors of Heidelberg recently did – there are no *grounds* for doing so.

6

To be true to my nature, which is *affirmative* and has dealings with contradiction and criticism only indirectly and when

* beauty is for the few.

compelled, I shall straightaway set down the three tasks for the sake of which one requires educators. One has to learn to *see*, one has to learn to *think*, one has to learn to *speak* and *write*: the end in all three is a noble culture. – Learning to *see* – habituating the eye to repose, to patience, to letting things come to it; learning to defer judgement, to investigate and comprehend the individual case in all its aspects. This is the *first* preliminary schooling in spirituality: *not* to react immediately to a stimulus, but to have the restraining, stock-taking instincts in one's control. Learning to *see*, as I understand it, is almost what is called in unphilosophical language 'strong will-power': the essence of it is precisely *not* to 'will', the *ability* to defer decision. All unspirituality, all vulgarity, is due to the incapacity to resist a stimulus – one *has* to react, one obeys every impulse. In many instances, such a compulsion is already morbidity, decline, a symptom of exhaustion – almost everything which unphilosophical crudity designates by the name 'vice' is merely this physiological incapacity *not* to react – A practical application of having learned to see: one will have become slow, mistrustful, resistant as a *learner* in general. In an attitude of hostile calm one will allow the strange, the *novel* of every kind to approach one first – one will draw one's hand back from it. To stand with all doors open, to prostrate oneself submissively before every petty fact, to be ever itching to mingle with, *plunge into* other people and other things, in short our celebrated modern 'objectivity', is bad taste, is ignoble *par excellence*. –

7

Learning to *think*: our schools no longer have any idea what this means. Even in our universities, even among students of philosophy themselves, the theory, the practice, the *vocation* of logic is beginning to die out. Read German books: no longer the remotest recollection that a technique, a plan of instruction, a will to mastery is required for thinking – that thinking has to be learned in the way dancing has to be learned, *as* a form of dancing. . . . Who among Germans still knows from experience that subtle thrill which the possession of intellectual *light feet* communicates to all the muscles! – A stiffly awkward air in intellectual matters, a clumsy hand in grasping – this is in so great a degree German that foreigners take it for the German nature in general. The German has no *fingers* for nuances. . . . That the Germans have so much as endured their philosophers, above all that most deformed conceptual cripple there has ever been, the *great* Kant, offers a good idea of German amenableness. – For *dancing* in any form cannot be divorced from a *noble education*, being able to dance with the feet, with concepts, with words: do I still have to say that one has to be able to dance with the *pen* – that *writing* has to be learned? – But at this point I should become a complete enigma to German readers . . .

Expeditions of an Untimely Man

1

My impossibles. – *Seneca*: or the toreador of virtue. – *Rousseau*: or the return to nature *in impuris naturalibus*.* – *Schiller*: or the Moral-Trumpeter of Säckingen.† – *Dante*: or the hyena which *poetizes* on graves. – *Kant*: or cant as intelligible character. – *Victor Hugo*: or the Pharos in the Sea of Absurdity. – *Liszt*: or the virtuoso – with women.‡ – *George Sand*: or *lactea ubertas,*§ in English: the milch cow with the 'fine style'. – *Michelet*: or enthusiasm which strips off the jacket. – *Carlyle*: or pessimism as indigestion. – *John Stuart Mill*: or offensive clarity. – *Les frères de Goncourt*: or the two Ajaxes struggling with Homer. Music by Offenbach. *Zola*: or 'delight in stinking'. –

2

Renan. – Theology, or the corruption of reason by 'original sin' (Christianity). Witness: Renan, who, whenever he risks a more general Yes or No, misses the point with painful regularity. He would like, for instance, to couple together *la science* and *la noblesse*; but *la science* belongs to democracy, that is patently obvious. He desires, with no little ambitiousness, to represent an aristocratism of the intellect: but at the same time he falls on his knees, and not only his knees, before its opposite, the *évangile des humbles*. . . . What avails all free-thinking, modernity, mockery and wry-necked flexibility, if

---

* in natural dirtiness.

† *Der Trompeter von Säckingen* (1853) by Joseph Viktor von Scheffel once enjoyed huge popularity in Germany; Viktor Nessler's opera based on it (1884) was also a popular success.

‡ *oder die Schule der Geläufigkeit – nach Weibern*. The joke is untranslatable: or the school of *Geläufigkeit* – after women. 'Geläufigkeit' means facility, skill (referring to Lizst's virtuosity as a pianist), but its root is 'laufen' = to run; and 'läufisch' means, among other things, lecherous.

§ milk in abundance.

one is still Christian, Catholic and even priest in one's bowels! Renan possesses his mode of inventiveness, just like a Jesuit or a father confessor, in devising means of seduction; his intellectuality does not lack the broad priestly smirk – like all priests, he becomes dangerous only when he loves. Nobody can equal him in deadly adoration. . . . This spirit of Renan, an *enervating* spirit, is one fatality more for poor, sick, feeble-willed France. –

3

Sainte-Beuve. – Nothing masculine in him; full of petty sullen wrath against all masculine spirit. Roams about, delicate, inquisitive, bored, eavesdropping – fundamentally a woman, with a woman's revengefulness and a woman's sensuousness. As psychologist a genius of *médisance*;* inexhaustibly rich in means for creating it; no one knows better how to mix poison with praise. Plebeian in the lowest instincts and related to Rousseau's *ressentiment*: *consequently* a romantic – for beneath all *romantisme* there grunts and thirsts Rousseau's instinct for revenge. A revolutionary, but kept tolerably in check by fear. Constrained in presence of everything possessing strength (public opinion, the Academy, the Court, even Port-Royal).† Embittered against all that is great in men and things, against all that believes in itself. Enough of a poet and semi-woman to feel greatness as power; constantly cringing, like the celebrated worm, because he constantly feels himself trodden on. As a critic without standards, steadiness or backbone, possessing the palate for a large variety of things of the cosmopolitan *libertin* but lacking the courage even to admit his *libertinage*. As a historian without philosophy, without the *power* of philosophical vision – for that reason rejecting, in all the main issues, the task of passing judgement, holding up 'objectivity'

* scandal.

† The headquarters in Paris of Jansenism, the doctrine that the human will is constitutionally incapable of goodness, and that salvation is therefore by free and undeserved grace. Sainte-Beuve wrote a celebrated history (1840–59) of the intellectual movement which grew up around Port-Royal.

as a mask. He comports himself differently, however, towards questions in which a delicate, experienced taste is the highest court of appeal: there he really does have the courage for himself, take pleasure in himself – there he is a *master*. – In some respects a preliminary form of Baudelaire. –

4

The *Imitatio Christi** is one of the books I cannot hold in my hand without experiencing a physiological resistance: it exhales a *parfum* of the 'eternal feminine'† for which one has to be French – or a Wagnerian. . . . This saint has a way of talking about love that makes even Parisiennes curious. – I am told that *cunningest* of Jesuits, A. Comte, who wanted to lead his Frenchmen to Rome via the *détour* of science, inspired himself with this book. I believe it: 'the religion of the heart' . . .

5

G. Eliot. – They have got rid of the Christian God, and now feel obliged to cling all the more firmly to Christian morality: that is *English* consistency, let us not blame it on little bluestockings *à la* Eliot. In England, in response to every little emancipation from theology one has to reassert one's position in a fear-inspiring manner as a moral fanatic. That is the *penance* one pays there. – With us it is different. When one gives up Christian belief one thereby deprives oneself of the *right* to Christian morality. For the latter is absolutely *not* self-evident: one must make this point clear again and again, in spite of English shallowpates. Christianity is a system, a consistently thought out and *complete* view of things. If one breaks out of it a fundamental idea, the belief in God, one thereby breaks the whole thing to pieces: one has nothing of

---

* *The Imitation of Christ*, a famous work attributed to the German mystic Thomas à Kempis (1379–1471).

† *das Ewig-Weibliche*, Goethe's coinage in the last lines of *Faust* ('The eternal-feminine draws us aloft'), is often the object of Nietzsche's mockery, apparently because he cannot see any meaning in it.

any consequence left in one's hands. Christianity presupposes that man does not know, *cannot* know what is good for him and what evil: he believes in God, who alone knows. Christian morality is a command: its origin is transcendental; it is beyond all criticism, all right to criticize; it possesses truth only if God is truth – it stands or falls with the belief in God. – If the English really do believe they know, of their own accord, 'intuitively', what is good and evil; if they consequently think they no longer have need of Christianity as a guarantee of morality; that is merely the *consequence* of the ascendancy of Christian evaluation and an expression of the *strength* and *depth* of this ascendancy: so that the origin of English morality has been forgotten, so that the highly conditional nature of its right to exist is no longer felt. For the Englishman morality is not yet a problem . . .

6

George Sand. – I have read the first *Lettres d'un voyageur*: like everything deriving from Rousseau false, artificial, fustian, exaggerated. I cannot endure this coloured-wallpaper style; nor the vulgar ambition to possess generous feelings. The worst, to be sure, is the female coquetting with male mannerisms, with the manners of ill-bred boys. – How cold she must have been withal, this insupportable authoress! She wound herself up like a clock – and wrote. . . . Cold, like Hugo, like Balzac, like all Romantics as soon as they started writing! And how complacently she liked to lie there, this prolific writing-cow, who had something German in the bad sense about her, like Rousseau her master, and who was in any case possible only with the decline of French taste! – But Renan respects her . . .

7

Moral code for psychologists. – No colportage psychology! Never observe *for the sake* of observing! That produces a false perspective, a squint, something forced and exaggerated. To experience from a *desire* to experience – that's no good. In experiencing, one *must* not look back towards oneself, or every glance becomes an 'evil eye'. A born psychologist instinctively guards against seeing for the sake of seeing; the same applies to the born painter. He never works 'from nature' – he leaves it to his instinct, his *camera obscura*, to sift and strain 'nature', the 'case', the 'experience'. . . . He is conscious only of the *universal*, the conclusion, the outcome: he knows nothing of that arbitrary abstraction from the individual case. – What will be the result if one does otherwise? Carries on colportage psychology in, for example, the manner of Parisian *romanciers* great and small? It is *that* sort of thing which as it were lies in wait for reality, which brings a handful of curiosities home each evening. . . . But just see what finally emerges – a pile of daubs, a mosaic at best, in any event something put together, restless, flashy. The worst in this kind is achieved by the Goncourts: they never put three sentences together which are not simply painful to the eye, the *psychologist's* eye. – Nature, artistically considered, is no model. It exaggerates, it distorts, it leaves gaps. Nature is *chance*. To study 'from nature' seems to me a bad sign: it betrays subjection, weakness, fatalism – this lying in the dust before *petits faits** is unworthy of a *complete* artist. Seeing *what is* – that pertains to a different species of spirit, the *anti-artistic*, the prosaic. One has to know *who* one is . . .

8

Towards a psychology of the artist. – For art to exist, for any sort of aesthetic activity or perception to exist, a certain physiological precondition is indispensable: *intoxication*. Intoxication must first have heightened the excitability of the entire machine: no art results before that happens. All kinds of intoxication, however different their origin, have the power to do this: above all, the intoxication of sexual excitement, the oldest and most primitive form of intoxication. Likewise the intoxication which comes in the train of all great desires, all strong emotions; the intoxication of feasting, of contest, of the brave deed, of victory, of all extreme agitation; the in-

* petty facts.

toxication of cruelty; intoxication in destruction; intoxication under certain meteorological influences, for example the intoxication of spring; or under the influence of narcotics; finally the intoxication of the will, the intoxication of an overloaded and distended will. – The essence of intoxication is the feeling of plenitude and increased energy. From out of this feeling one gives to things, one *compels* them to take, one rapes them – one calls this procedure *idealizing*. Let us get rid of a prejudice here: idealization does *not* consist, as is commonly believed, in a subtracting or deducting of the petty and secondary. A tremendous *expulsion* of the principal features rather is the decisive thing, so that thereupon the others too disappear.

9

In this condition one enriches everything out of one's own abundance: what one sees, what one desires, one sees swollen, pressing, strong, overladen with energy. The man in this condition transforms things until they mirror his power – until they are reflections of his perfection. This *compulsion* to transform into the perfect is – art. Even all that which he is not becomes for him nonetheless part of his joy in himself; in art, man takes delight in himself as perfection. – It would be permissible to imagine an antithetical condition, a specific anti-artisticality of instinct – a mode of being which impoverishes and attenuates things and makes them consumptive. And history is in fact rich in such anti-artists, in such starvelings of life, who necessarily have to take things to themselves, impoverish them, make them *leaner*. This is, for example, the case with the genuine Christian, with Pascal for example: a Christian who is at the same time an artist *does not exist.* . . . Let no one be childish and cite Raphael as an objection, or some homoeopathic Christian of the nineteenth century: Raphael said Yes, Raphael *did* Yes, consequently Raphael was not a Christian . . .

10

What is the meaning of the antithetical concepts *Apollinian* and *Dionysian*, both conceived as forms of intoxication, which I introduced into aesthetics?* – Apollinian intoxication alerts above all the eye, so that it acquires power of vision. The painter, the sculptor, the epic poet are visionaries *par excellence*. In the Dionysian state, on the other hand, the entire emotional system is alerted and intensified: so that it discharges all its powers of representation, imitation, transfiguration, transmutation, every kind of mimicry and play-acting, conjointly. The essential thing remains the facility of the metamorphosis, the incapacity *not* to react (– in a similar way to certain types of hysteric, who also assume *any* role at the slightest instigation). It is impossible for the Dionysian man not to understand any suggestion of whatever kind, he ignores no signal from the emotions, he possesses to the highest degree the instinct for understanding and divining, just as he possesses the art of communication to the highest degree. He enters into every skin, into every emotion; he is continually transforming himself. – Music, as we understand it today, is likewise a collective arousal and discharging of the emotions, but for all that only a vestige of a much fuller emotional world of expression, a mere residuum of Dionysian histrionicism. To make music possible as a separate art one had to immobilize a number of senses, above all the muscular sense (at least relatively: for all rhythm still speaks to our muscles to a certain extent): so that man no longer straightway imitates and represents bodily everything he feels. Nonetheless, *that* is the true Dionysian normal condition, at least its original condition: music is the gradually-achieved specialization of this at the expense of the most closely related faculties.

11

The actor, the mime, the dancer, the musician, the lyric poet are fundamentally related in their instincts and essentially one,

* In the *Birth of Tragedy*.

only gradually specialized and separated from one another – even to the point of opposition. The lyric poet stayed united longest with the musician, the actor with the dancer. – The *architect* represents neither a Dionysian nor an Apollinian condition: here it is the mighty act of will, the will which moves mountains, the intoxication of the strong will, which demands artistic expression. The most powerful men have always inspired the architects; the architect has always been influenced by power. Pride, victory over weight and gravity, the will to power, seek to render themselves visible in a building; architecture is a kind of rhetoric of power, now persuasive, even cajoling in form, now bluntly imperious. The highest feeling of power and security finds expression in that which possesses *grand style*. Power which no longer requires proving; which disdains to please; which is slow to answer; which is conscious of no witnesses around it; which lives oblivious of the existence of any opposition; which reposes in *itself*, fatalistic, a law among laws: *that* is what speaks of itself in the form of grand style. –

12

I have read the life of *Thomas Carlyle*, that unwitting and involuntary farce, that heroical-moralistical interpretation of dyspepsia. – Carlyle, a man of strong words and attitudes, a rhetorician from *necessity*, continually agitated by the desire for a strong faith *and* the feeling of incapacity for it (– in this a typical Romantic!) The desire for a strong faith is *not* the proof of a strong faith, rather the opposite. *If one has it* one may permit oneself the beautiful luxury of scepticism: one is secure enough, firm enough, fixed enough for it. Carlyle deafens something within him by the *fortissimo* of his reverence for men of strong faith and by his rage against the less single-minded: he *requires* noise. A continual passionate *dishonesty* towards himself – that is his *proprium*, because of that he is and will remain interesting. – To be sure, in England he is admired precisely on account of his honesty. . . . Well, that is English; and, considering the English are the nation of consummate cant, even appropriate and not merely understandable. Fundamentally, Carlyle is an English atheist who wants to be honoured for *not* being one.

13

Emerson. – Much more enlightened, adventurous, multifarious, refined than Carlyle; above all, happier. ... Such a man as instinctively feeds on pure ambrosia and leaves alone the indigestible in things. Compared with Carlyle a man of taste. – Carlyle, who had a great affection for him, nevertheless said of him: 'He does not give *us* enough to bite on': which may be truly said, but not to the detriment of Emerson. – Emerson possesses that good-natured and quick-witted cheerfulness that discourages all earnestness; he has absolutely no idea how old he is or how young he will be – he could say of himself, in the words of Lope de Vega: *'yo me sucedo a mi mismo'.** His spirit is always finding reasons for being contented and even grateful; and now and then he verges on the cheerful transcendence of that worthy gentleman who, returning from an amorous rendezvous *tamquam re bene gesta,* said gratefully: *'Ut desint vires, tamen est laudanda voluptas.'†*

14

Anti-Darwin. – As regards the celebrated 'struggle for *life',* it seems to me for the present to have been rather asserted than proved. It does occur, but as the exception; the general aspect of life is *not* hunger and distress, but rather wealth, luxury, even absurd prodigality – where there is a struggle it is a struggle for *power.* ... One should not mistake Malthus for nature. – Supposing, however, that this struggle exists – and it does indeed occur – its outcome is the reverse of that desired

---

* I am my own successor.

† ... that worthy gentleman who, returning from an amorous rendezvous as if things had gone well, said gratefully: 'Though the power be lacking, the lust is praiseworthy.' *'Voluptas'* replaces the usual *'voluntas'* = will.

by the school of Darwin, of that which one *ought* perhaps to desire with them: namely, the defeat of the stronger, the more privileged, the fortunate exceptions. Species do *not* grow more perfect: the weaker dominate the strong again and again – the reason being they are the great majority, and they are also *cleverer*. . . . Darwin forgot the mind (– that is English!): *the weak possess more mind.* . . . To acquire mind one must need mind – one loses it when one no longer needs it. He who possesses strength divests himself of mind (– 'let it depart!' they think today in Germany, '– the *Reich* will still be ours.' . . .)* One will see that under mind I include foresight, patience, dissimulation, great self-control, and all that is mimicry (this last includes a great part of what is called virtue).

15

Psychologist's casuistry. This man is a human psychologist: what does he really study men for? He wants to gain little advantages over them, or big ones too – he is a politician! . . . This other man is also a human psychologist: and you say he wants nothing for himself, that he is 'impersonal'. Take a closer look! Perhaps he wants an even *worse* advantage: to feel himself superior to men, to have the right to look down on them, no longer to confuse himself with them. This 'impersonal' man is a *despiser* of men: and the former is a more humane species, which may even be clear from his appearance. At least he thinks himself equal to others, he *involves* himself with others . . .

16

The *psychological taste* of the Germans seems to me to be called in question by a whole series of instances which modesty forbids me to enumerate. There is one instance, however, which offers me a grand opportunity for establishing my thesis: I bear the Germans a grudge for their having blundered

---

* Refers to the last lines of Luther's hymn *'Ein' feste Burg'* – where, however, what is to be let depart is the things of this world and the *Reich* means the kingdom of Heaven.

over *Kant* and his 'backdoor philosophy', as I call it – this was *not* the pattern of intellectual integrity. – Another thing I loathe to hear is an infamous 'and': the Germans say 'Goethe *and* Schiller' – I am afraid they say 'Schiller and Goethe'. . . . Don't people *know* this Schiller yet? – There are even worse 'ands'; I have heard 'Schopenhauer *and* Hartmann' with my own ears, though only among university professors, admittedly . . .

17

The most spiritual human beings, assuming they are the most courageous, also experience by far the most painful tragedies: but it is precisely for this reason that they honour life, because it brings against them its most formidable weapons.

18

On the subject of 'intellectual conscience'. – Nothing seems to me to be rarer today than genuine hypocrisy. I greatly suspect that this plant finds the mild atmosphere of our culture unendurable. Hypocrisy has its place in the ages of strong belief: in which even when one is *compelled* to exhibit a different belief one does not abandon the belief one already has. Today one does abandon it; or, which is even more common, one acquires a second belief – one remains *honest* in any event. Beyond doubt, a very much larger number of convictions are possible today than formerly: possible, that means permitted, that means *harmless*. That is the origin of self-tolerance. – Self-tolerance permits one to possess several convictions; these conciliate one another – they take care, as all the world does today, not to compromise themselves. How does one compromise oneself today? By being consistent. By going in a straight line. By being less than ambiguous. By being genuine. . . . I greatly fear that modern man is simply too indolent for certain vices: so that they are actually dying out. All evil which is dependent on strong will – and perhaps there is nothing evil without strength of will – is degenerating, in our tepid atmosphere, into virtue. . . . The few hypocrites I have known impersonated hypocrisy: they were, like virtually every tenth man nowadays, actors. –

19

*Beautiful and ugly.** – Nothing is so conditional, let us say *circumscribed*, as our feeling for the beautiful. Anyone who tried to divorce it from man's pleasure in man would at once find the ground give way beneath him. The 'beautiful in itself' is not even a concept, merely a phrase. In the beautiful, man sets himself up as the standard of perfection; in select cases he worships himself in it. A species *cannot* do otherwise than affirm itself alone in this manner. Its *deepest* instinct, that of self-preservation and self-aggrandizement, is still visible in such sublimated forms. Man believes that the world itself is filled with beauty – he *forgets* that it is he who has created it. He alone has bestowed beauty upon the world – alas! only a very human, all too human beauty. . . . Man really mirrors himself in things, that which gives him back his own reflection he considers beautiful: the judgement 'beautiful' is his *conceit of his species*. . . . For a tiny suspicion whispers into the sceptic's ear: is the world actually made beautiful because *man* finds it so? Man has *humanized* the world: that is all. But there is nothing, absolutely nothing, to guarantee to us that *man* constitutes the model for the beautiful. Who knows what figure he would cut in the eyes of a higher arbiter of taste? Perhaps a presumptuous one? perhaps even risible? perhaps a little arbitrary? . . . 'O Dionysus, divine one, why do you pull my ears?' Ariadne once asked her philosophical lover during one of those celebrated dialogues on Naxos.† 'I find a kind of humour in your ears, Ariadne: why are they not longer?'

20

Nothing is beautiful, only man: on this piece of naïvety rests all aesthetics, it is the *first* truth of aesthetics. Let us immediately

* *Schön und hässlich* is the German translation of Macbeth's witches' 'fair and foul'.

† Fragmentary sketches by Nietzsche published after his death, i.e. long after this reference to them.

add its second: nothing is ugly but *degenerate* man – the domain of aesthetic judgement is therewith defined. – Reckoned physiologically, everything ugly weakens and afflicts man. It recalls decay, danger, impotence; he actually suffers a loss of energy in its presence. The effect of the ugly can be measured with a dynamometer. Whenever man feels in any way depressed, he senses the proximity of something 'ugly'. His feeling of power, his will to power, his courage, his pride – they decline with the ugly, they increase with the beautiful. . . . In the one case as in the other *we draw a conclusion*: its premises have been accumulated in the instincts in tremendous abundance. The ugly is understood as a sign and symptom of degeneration: that which recalls degeneration, however remotely, produces in us the judgement 'ugly'. Every token of exhaustion, of heaviness, of age, of weariness, every kind of unfreedom, whether convulsive or paralytic, above all the smell, colour and shape of dissolution, of decomposition, though it be attenuated to the point of being no more than a symbol – all this calls forth the same reaction, the value judgement 'ugly'. A feeling of *hatred* then springs up; what is man then hating? But the answer admits of no doubt: the *decline of his type*. He hates then from out of the profoundest instinct of his species; there is horror, foresight, profundity, far-seeing vision in this hatred – it is the profoundest hatred there is. It is for its sake that art is *profound* . . .

21

Schopenhauer. – Schopenhauer, the last German of any consequence (– who is a *European* event like Goethe, like Hegel, like Heinrich Heine, and *not merely* a parochial, a 'national' one), is for a psychologist a case of the first order: namely, as a mendacious attempt of genius to marshal, in aid of a nihilistic total devaluation of life, the very counter-instances, the great self-affirmations of the 'will to live', the exuberant forms of life. He interpreted in turn *art*, heroism, genius, beauty, grand sympathy, knowledge, the will to truth, tragedy, as phenomena consequent upon the 'denial' of or the thirst to deny the 'will' – the greatest piece of psychological false-coinage in history, Christianity alone excepted. Looked at more closely he is in this merely the heir of the Christian interpretation: but with this difference, that he knew how to make what Christianity had *rejected*, the great cultural facts of mankind, and *approve* of them from a Christian, that is to say nihilistic, point of view (– namely as roads to 'redemption', as preliminary forms of 'redemption', as stimulants of the thirst for 'redemption' . . .).

22

To take a particular instance: Schopenhauer speaks of *beauty* with a melancholy ardour – why, in the last resort? Because he sees in it a *bridge* upon which one may pass over, or acquire a thirst to pass over. . . . It is to him redemption from the 'will' for minutes at a time – it lures on to redemption for ever. . . . He values it especially as redeemer from the 'focus of the will', from sexuality – in beauty he sees the procreative impulse *denied*. . . . Singular saint! Someone contradicts you, and I fear it is nature. *To what end* is there beauty at all in the sounds, colours, odours, rhythmic movements of nature? what *makes* beauty *appear*? – Fortunately a philosopher also contradicts him. No less an authority than the divine Plato (– so Schopenhauer himself calls him) maintains a different thesis: that all beauty incites to procreation – that precisely this is the *proprium* of its effect, from the most sensual regions up into the most spiritual . . .

23

Plato goes further. He says, with an innocence for which one must be Greek and not 'Christian', that there would be no Platonic philosophy at all if Athens had not possessed such beautiful youths: it was the sight of them which first plunged the philosopher's soul into an erotic whirl and allowed it no rest until it had implanted the seed of all high things into so beautiful a soil. Another singular saint! – one doesn't believe one's ears, even supposing one believes Plato. One sees, at least, that philosophizing was *different* in Athens, above all public. Nothing is less Greek than the conceptual cobweb-spinning of a hermit, *amor intellectualis dei** in the manner of Spinoza. Philosophy in the manner of Plato should rather be defined as an erotic contest, as a further development and inward intensification of the old agonal gymnastics and their *presuppositions*. . . . What finally emerged from this philosophical eroticism of Plato? A new artistic form of the Greek agon, dialectics. – I further recall, *opposing* Schopenhauer and to the honour of Plato, that the entire higher culture and literature of *classical* France also grew up on the soil of sexual interest. One may seek everywhere in it for gallantry, sensuality, sexual contest, 'woman' – one will never seek in vain . . .

24

L'art pour l'art.† – The struggle against *purpose* in art is always a struggle against the *moralizing* tendency in art, against the subordination of art to morality. *L'art pour l'art* means: 'the devil take morality!' – But this very hostility betrays that moral prejudice is still dominant. When one has excluded from art the purpose of moral preaching and human improvement it by no means follows that art is completely purposeless, goalless, meaningless, in short *l'art pour l'art* – a snake biting its own tail. 'Rather no purpose at all than a moral purpose!' – thus speaks mere passion. A psychologist asks on the other hand: what does all art do? does it not praise? does it not glorify? does it not select? does it not highlight? By doing all this it *strengthens* or *weakens* certain valuations. . . . Is this no more than an incidental? an accident? Something in which the instinct of the artist has no part whatever? Or is it not rather the prerequisite for the artist's being an artist at all. . . . Is his basic instinct directed towards art, or is it not rather directed towards the meaning of art, which is *life*? towards *a desideratum of life*? – Art is the great stimulus to life: how could it be thought purposeless, aimless, *l'art pour l'art*? One question remains: art also brings to light much that is ugly, hard,

* intellectual love of God.   † Art for art's sake.

questionable in life – does it not thereby seem to suffer from life? – And there have indeed been philosophers who lent it this meaning: Schopenhauer taught that the whole object of art was to 'liberate from the will', and he revered tragedy because its greatest function was to 'dispose one to resignation'. – But this – as I have already intimated – is pessimist's perspective and 'evil eye' – : one must appeal to the artists themselves. *What does the tragic artist communicate of himself?* Does he not display precisely the condition of *fearlessness* in the face of the fearsome and questionable? – This condition itself is a high desideratum: he who knows it bestows on it the highest honours. He communicates it, he *has* to communicate it if he is an artist, a genius of communication. Bravery and composure in the face of a powerful enemy, great hardship, a problem that arouses aversion – it is this *victorious* condition which the tragic artist singles out, which he glorifies. In the face of tragedy the warlike in our soul celebrates its Saturnalias; whoever is accustomed to suffering, whoever seeks out suffering, the *heroic* man extols his existence by means of tragedy – for him alone does the tragic poet pour this draught of sweetest cruelty. –

25

To put up with men, to keep open house in one's heart – this is liberal, but no more than liberal. One knows hearts which are capable of *noble* hospitality, which have curtained windows and closed shutters: they keep their best rooms empty. Why do they so? – Because they await guests with whom one does *not* have to 'put up' . . .

26

We no longer have a sufficiently high estimate of ourselves when we communicate. Our true experiences are not garrulous. They could not communicate themselves if they wanted to: they lack words. We have already grown beyond whatever we have words for. In all talking there lies a grain of contempt. Speech, it seems, was devised only for the average, medium, communicable. The speaker has already *vulgarized* himself by speaking. – From a moral code for deaf-mutes and other philosophers.

27

'This picture is enchanting fair!'* ... The literary woman, unsatisfied, agitated, desolate in heart and entrails, listening every minute with painful curiosity to the imperative which whispers from the depths of her organism '*aut liberi aut libri*':† the literary woman, cultured enough to understand the voice of nature even when it speaks Latin, and on the other hand vain enough and enough of a goose to say secretly to herself in French '*je me verrai, je me lirai, je m'extasierai et je dirai: Possible, que j'aie eu tant d'esprit?*' ...‡

28

The 'impersonal' take the floor. – 'We find nothing easier than being wise, patient, superior. We drip with the oil of forbearance and sympathy, we are absurdly just, we forgive everything. For that very reason we ought to discipline ourselves a little; for that very reason we ought to *cultivate* a little emotion, a little emotional vice, from time to time. It may be hard for us; and among ourselves we may perhaps laugh at the appearance we thus present. But what of that! We no longer have any other mode of self-overcoming available to us: this is *our* asceticism, *our* penance'. ... *Becoming personal* – the virtue of the 'impersonal' ...

29

From a doctorate exam. – 'What is the task of all higher education?' – To turn a man into a machine. – 'By what means?' –

* The opening line of an aria in Mozart's *The Magic Flute*.
† children or books.
‡ I shall look at myself, I shall read myself, I shall delight myself and I shall say: Can I really have had so much wit?

He has to learn how to feel bored. – 'How is that achieved?' – Through the concept of duty. – 'Who is his model?' – The philologist: he teaches how to *grind*.* – 'Who is the perfect man?' – The civil servant. – 'Which philosophy provides the best formula for the civil servant?' – Kant's: the civil servant as thing in itself set as judge over the civil servant as appearance. –

30

The right to stupidity. – The wearied and slow-breathing worker, good-natured, letting things take their course: this typical figure, who is now, in the Age of Work (*and* of the ' *Reich*'!–), encountered in all classes of society, is today laying claim even to *art*, including the book and above all the journal – how much more to the beauties of nature, to Italy. . . . The man of the evening, with the 'wild instincts lulled to sleep' of which Faust speaks,† requires the health resort, the seaside, the glaciers, Bayreuth.‡ . . . In ages like this, art has a right to *pure folly*§ – as a kind of holiday for the spirit, the wits and the heart. Wagner understood that. *Pure folly* is a restorative . . .

31

Another problem of diet. – The means by which Julius Caesar defended himself against sickliness and headache: tremendous marches, the simplest form of living, uninterrupted sojourn in the open air, continuous toil – these, broadly speaking, are the universal preservative and protective measures against the extreme vulnerability of that subtle machine working at the highest pressure which is called genius. –

* *ochsen:* to work hard, slave – also to cram, study hard.

† In Goethe's *Faust,* Part 1, Scene 3.

‡ The seat of the Wagner Festival.

§ Parsifal, eponymous hero of Wagner's last opera, is described as a pure, i.e. chaste, fool (*reine Tor*) whose naïvety is proof against temptation of every kind. Nietzsche considered the plot of *Parsifal* preposterous and persistently uses the phrase *'reine Torheit'* (pure folly) in the sense of *complete* folly.

32

The immoralist speaks. – Nothing offends a philosopher's taste *more* than man *when he expresses desires.* ... When the philosopher sees man only in his activity, when he sees this bravest, cunningest, toughest of animals straying even into labyrinthine calamities, how admirable man seems to him! He encourages him. ... But the philosopher despises desiring man, and the 'desirable' man too – he despises all the desiderata, all the *ideals* of man. If a philosopher could be a nihilist, he would be one because he finds nothingness behind all the ideals of men. Or not even nothingness merely – but only the worthless, the absurd, the sick, the cowardly, the weary, dregs of all kinds from the cup of his life *after he has drained it.* ... How does it come about that man, so admirable as a reality, deserves no respect when he expresses desires? Does he have to atone for being so able as a reality? Does he have to compensate for his activity, for the exertion of will and hand involved in all activity, with a relaxation in the imaginary and absurd? – The history of his desiderata has hitherto been the *partie honteuse** of man: one should take care not to read too long in it. What justifies man is his reality – it will justify him eternally. How much more valuable an actual man is compared with any sort of merely desired, dreamed of, odious lie of a man? with any sort of *ideal* man? ... And it is only the ideal man who offends the philosopher's taste.

33

The natural value of egoism. – The value of egoism depends on the physiological value of him who possesses it: it can be very valuable, it can be worthless and contemptible. Every individual may be regarded as representing the ascending or descending line of life. When one has decided which, one has thereby established a canon for the value of his egoism. If he represents the ascending line his value is in fact extraordinary – and for the sake of the life-collective, which with him takes a

* shameful part.

step *forward*, the care expended on his preservation, on the creation of optimum conditions for him, may even be extreme. For the individual, the 'single man', as people and philosophers have hitherto understood him, is an error: he does not constitute a separate entity, an atom, a 'link in the chain', something merely inherited from the past – he constitutes the entire *single* line 'man' up to and including himself. . . . If he represents the descending development, decay, chronic degeneration, sickening (– sickness is, broadly speaking, already a phenomenon consequent upon decay, *not* the cause of it), then he can be accorded little value, and elementary fairness demands that he *take away* as little as possible from the well-constituted. He is no better than a parasite on them . . .

34

Christian and anarchist. – When the anarchist, as the mouthpiece of *declining* strata of society, demands with righteous indignation 'his rights', 'justice', 'equal rights', he is only acting under the influence of his want of culture, which prevents his understanding *why* he is really suffering – in *what respect* he is impoverished, in life. . . . A cause-creating drive is powerful within him: someone must be to blame for his feeling vile. . . . His 'righteous indignation' itself already does him good; every poor devil finds pleasure in scolding - it gives him a little of the intoxication of power. Even complaining and wailing can give life a charm for the sake of which one endures it: there is a small dose of *revenge* in every complaint, one reproaches those who are different for one's feeling vile, sometimes even with one's being vile, as if they had perpetrated an injustice or possessed an *impermissible* privilege. 'If I am *canaille*, you ought to be so too': on the basis of this logic one makes revolutions. – Complaining is never of any use: it comes from weakness. Whether one attributes one's feeling vile to others or to *oneself* – the Socialist does the former, the Christian for example the latter – makes no essential difference. What is common to both, and *unworthy* in both, is that someone has to be to *blame* for the fact that one suffers – in short, that the sufferer prescribes for himself the honey of revenge as a medicine for his suffering. The objectives of this thirst for revenge as a thirst for *pleasure* vary according to circumstances: the sufferer finds occasions everywhere for cooling his petty revengefulness – if he is a Christian, to say it again, he finds them in *himself*. . . . The Christian and the anarchist – both are *décadents*. – And when the Christian condemns, calumniates and befouls the '*world*', he does so from the same instinct from which the Socialist worker condemns, calumniates and befouls *society*: even the 'Last Judgement' is still the sweet consolation of revenge – the revolution, such as the Socialist worker too anticipates, only conceived of as somewhat more distant. . . . Even the 'Beyond' – why a Beyond if not as a means of befouling the Here-and-Now? . . .

35

A criticism of décadence morality. – An 'altruistic' morality, a morality under which egoism *languishes* – is under all circumstances a bad sign. This applies to individuals, it applies especially to peoples. The best are lacking when egoism begins to be lacking. To choose what is harmful to *oneself*, to be *attracted* by 'disinterested' motives, almost constitutes the formula for *décadence*. 'Not to seek *one's own* advantage' – that is merely a moral figleaf for a quite different, namely physiological fact: 'I no longer know how to *find* my advantage'. . . . Disgregation of the instincts! – Man is finished when he becomes altruistic. – Instead of saying simply '*I* am no longer worth anything', the moral lie in the mouth of the *décadent* says: 'Nothing is worth anything – *life* is not worth anything'. . . . Such a judgement represents, after all, a grave danger, it is contagious – on the utterly morbid soil of society it soon grows up luxuriously, now in the form of religion (Christianity), now in that of philosophy (Schopenhauerism). In some circumstances the vapours of such a poison-tree jungle sprung up out of putrefaction can poison *life* for years ahead, for thousands of years ahead . . .

36

A moral code for physicians. – The invalid is a parasite on society. In a certain state it is indecent to go on living. To vegetate on in cowardly dependence on physicians and medicaments after the meaning of life, the *right* to life, has been lost ought to entail the profound contempt of society. Physicians, in their turn, ought to be the communicators of this contempt – not prescriptions, but every day a fresh dose of *disgust* with their patients. ... To create a new responsibility, that of the physician, in all cases in which the highest interest of life, of *ascending* life, demands the most ruthless suppression and sequestration of degenerating life – for example in determining the right to reproduce, the right to be born, the right to live. ... To die proudly when it is no longer possible to live proudly. Death of one's own free choice, death at the proper time, with a clear head and with joyfulness, consummated in the midst of children and witnesses: so that an actual leave-taking is possible while he who is leaving *is still there*, likewise an actual evaluation of what has been desired and what achieved in life, an *adding-up* of life – all of this in contrast to the pitiable and horrible comedy Christianity has made of the hour of death. One should never forget of Christianity that it has abused the weakness of the dying to commit conscience-rape and even the mode of death to formulate value judgements on men and the past! – Here, every cowardice of prejudice notwithstanding, it is above all a question of establishing the correct, that is physiological evaluation of so-called *natural* death: which is, after all, also only an 'unnatural' death, an act of suicide. One perishes by no one but oneself. Only 'natural' death is death for the most contemptible reasons, an unfree death, a death at the *wrong* time, a coward's death. From love of *life* one ought to desire to die differently from this: freely, consciously, not accidentally, not suddenly overtaken. ... Finally, a piece of advice for *messieurs* the pessimists and other *décadents*. We have no power to prevent ourselves being born: but we can rectify this error – for it is sometimes an error. When one *does away with* oneself one does

the most estimable thing possible: one thereby almost deser
to live. . . . Society – what am I saying! *life* itself derives mo.
advantage from that than from any sort of 'life' spent in
renunciation, green-sickness and other virtues – one has
freed others from having to endure one's sight, one has
removed an *objection* from life. . . . Pessimism, *pur, vert,**
proves itself only by the self-negation of *messieurs* the pessimists:
one must take their logic a step further, and not deny life
merely in 'will and idea', as Schopenhauer did – one must
first of all deny Schopenhauer. . . . Pessimism, by the by, however
contagious it may be, nevertheless does not add to the morbidity of an age or a race in general: it is the expression of this
morbidity. One succumbs to it as one succumbs to cholera:
one's constitution must already be sufficiently morbid.
Pessimism does not of itself make a single additional *décadent*;
I recall that statistics show that the years in which cholera
rages do not differ from other years in the total number of
deaths.

37

Whether we have grown more moral. – As was only to be expected,
the whole *ferocity* of the moral stupidity which, as is well
known, is considered morality as such in Germany, has
launched itself against my concept 'beyond good and evil':
I could tell some pretty stories about it. Above all, I was
invited to reflect on the 'undeniable superiority' of our age in
moral judgement, our real *advance* in this respect: compared
with *us*, a Cesare Borgia was certainly not to be set up as a
'higher man', as a kind of *superman*, in the way I set him up.
. . . A Swiss editor, that of the 'Bund', went so far – n: without expressing his admiration of the courage for so ha dous
an enterprise – as to 'understand' that the meaning of work
lay in a proposal to abolish all decent feeling. Much liged!†
– by way of reply I permit myself to raise the qu whether
we have really grown more moral. That all the wo lieves so
is already an objection to it. . . . We mod hen, very

* pure, raw.
† *Sehr verbunden!* – a play on the name of '   d'.

...icate, very vulnerable and paying and receiving considera-
...on in a hundred ways, imagine in fact that this sensitive
humanity which we represent, this *achieved* unanimity in forbearance, in readiness to help, in mutual trust, is a positive
advance, that with this we have gone far beyond the men of
the Renaissance. But every age thinks in this way, *has* to think
in this way. What is certain is that we would not dare to place
ourselves in Renaissance circumstances, or even imagine ourselves in them: our nerves could not endure that reality, not to
speak of our muscles. This incapacity, however, demonstrates,
not an advance, but only a different, a more belated constitution, a weaker, more delicate, more vulnerable one, out of
which is necessarily engendered a morality *which is full of
consideration*. If we think away our delicacy and belatedness, our
physiological ageing, then our morality of 'humanization' too
loses its value at once – no morality has any value in itself – :
we would even despise it. On the other hand, let us be in no
doubt that we modern men, with our thick padding of
humanity which dislikes to give the slightest offence, would
provide the contemporaries of Cesare Borgia with a side-
splitting comedy. We are, in fact, involuntarily funny beyond
all measure, we with our modern 'virtues'. . . . The decay of
our hostile and mistrust-arousing instincts – and that is what
constitutes our 'advance' – represents only one of the
effects attending our general decay of *vitality*: it costs a hundred
times more effort, more foresight, to preserve so dependent,
so late an existence as we are. Here everyone helps everyone
else, here everyone is to a certain degree an invalid and everyone a nurse. This is then called 'virtue' – : among men who
knew a different kind of life, a fuller, more prodigal, more
overflowing life, it would be called something else: 'cowardice', perhaps, 'pitiableness', 'old woman's morality'. . . . Our
softening of customs – this is my thesis, my *innovation* if you
like – is a consequence of decline; stern and frightful customs
can, conversely, be a consequence of a superabundance of life.
For in the latter case much may be risked, much demanded
and much squandered. What was formerly a spice of life
would be poison to us. . . . We are likewise too old, too belated,

to be capable of indifference – also a form of strength: our morality of pity, against which I was the first to warn, that which one might call *l'impressionisme morale*, is one more expression of the physiological over-excitability pertaining to everything *décadent*. That movement which with Schopenhauer's *morality of pity* attempted to present itself as scientific – a very unsuccessful attempt! – is the actual *décadence* movement in morality; as such it is profoundly related to Christian morality. Strong ages, *noble* cultures, see in pity, in 'love of one's neighbour', in a lack of self and self-reliance, something contemptible. – Ages are to be assessed according to their *positive forces* – and by this assessment the age of the Renaissance, so prodigal and so fateful, appears as the last *great* age, and we, we moderns with our anxious care for ourselves and love of our neighbour, with our virtues of work, of unpretentiousness, of fair play, of scientificality – acquisitive, economical, machine-minded – appear as a *weak* age.... Our virtues are conditioned, are *demanded* by our weakness. ... 'Equality', a certain actual rendering similar of which the theory of 'equal rights' is only the expression, belongs essentially to decline: the chasm between man and man, class and class, the multiplicity of types, the will to be oneself, to stand out – that which I call *pathos of distance* – characterizes every *strong* age. The tension, the range between the extremes is today growing less and less – the extremes themselves are finally obliterated to the point of similarity. ... All our political theories *and* state constitutions, the 'German *Reich*' certainly not excluded, are consequences, necessary effects of decline; the unconscious influence of *décadence* has gained ascendancy even over the ideals of certain of the sciences. My objection to the whole of sociology in England and France is that it knows from experience only the *decaying forms* of society and takes its own decaying instincts with perfect innocence as the *norm* of sociological value judgement. *Declining* life, the diminution of all organizing power, that is to say the power of separating, of opening up chasms, of ranking above and below, formulates itself in the sociology of today as the *ideal*. ... Our Socialists are *décadents*, but Mr Herbert Spencer is also a *décadent* – he sees in the victory of altruism something desirable! . . .

38

My conception of freedom. – The value of a thing sometimes lies not in what one attains with it, but in what one pays for it – what it *costs* us. I give an example. Liberal institutions immediately cease to be liberal as soon as they are attained: subsequently there is nothing more thoroughly harmful to freedom than liberal institutions. One knows, indeed, *what* they bring about: they undermine the will to power, they are the levelling of mountain and valley exalted to a moral principle, they make small, cowardly and smug – it is the herd animal which triumphs with them every time. Liberalism: in plain words, *reduction to the herd animal*. . . . As long as they are still being fought for, these same institutions produce quite different effects; they then in fact promote freedom mightily. Viewed more closely, it is war which produces these effects, war *for* liberal institutions which as war permits the *illiberal* instincts to endure. And war is a training in freedom. For what is freedom? That one has the will to self-responsibility. That one preserves the distance which divides us. That one has become more indifferent to hardship, toil, privation, even to life. That one is ready to sacrifice men to one's cause, oneself not excepted. Freedom means that the manly instincts that delight in war and victory have gained mastery over the other instincts – for example, over the instinct for 'happiness'. The man *who has become free* – and how much more the *mind* that has become free – spurns the contemptible sort of well-being dreamed of by shopkeepers, Christians, cows, women, Englishmen and other democrats. The free man is a *warrior.* – How is freedom measured, in individuals as in nations? By the resistance which has to be overcome, by the effort it costs to stay *aloft*. One would have to seek the highest type of free man where the greatest resistance is constantly being overcome: five steps from tyranny, near the threshold of the danger of servitude. This is true psychologically when one understands by 'tyrants' pitiless and dreadful instincts, to combat which demands the maximum of authority and discipline towards oneself – finest type Julius Caesar – ; it is also true politically: one has only to look at history. The nations which were worth something, which *became* worth something, never became so under liberal institutions: it was *great danger* which made of them something deserving reverence, danger which first teaches us to know our resources, our virtues, our shield and spear, our *spirit* – which *compels* us to be strong. . . . *First* principle: one must need strength, otherwise one will never have it. – Those great forcing-houses for strong human beings, for the strongest kind there has ever been, the aristocratic communities of the pattern of Rome and Venice, understood freedom in precisely the sense in which I understand the word 'freedom': as something one has and does *not* have, something one *wants*, something one *conquers* . . .

39

Criticism of modernity. – Our institutions are no longer fit for anything: everyone is unanimous about that. But the fault lies not in them but in *us*. Having lost all the instincts out of which institutions grow, we are losing the institutions themselves, because *we* are no longer fit for them. Democracy has always been the declining form of the power to organize: I have already, in *Human, All Too Human*, characterized modern democracy, together with its imperfect manifestations such as the 'German *Reich*', as the *decaying form* of the state. For institutions to exist there must exist the kind of will, instinct, imperative which is anti-liberal to the point of malice: the will to tradition, to authority, to centuries-long responsibility, to *solidarity* between succeeding generations backwards and forewards *in infinitum*. If this will is present, there is established something such as the *Imperium Romanum*: or such as Russia, the *only* power today which has durability in it, which can wait, which can still promise something – Russia, the antithesis of that pitiable European petty-state politics and nervousness which with the foundation of the German *Reich* has entered a critical phase. . . . The entire West has lost those instincts out of

93

which institutions grow, out of which the *future* grows: perhaps nothing goes so much against the grain of its 'modern spirit' as this. One lives for today, one lives very fast – one lives very irresponsibly: it is precisely this which one calls 'freedom'. That which *makes* institutions institutions is despised, hated, rejected: whenever the word 'authority' is so much as heard one believes oneself in danger of a new slavery. The *décadence* in the valuating instinct of our politicians, our political parties, goes so deep that *they instinctively prefer* that which leads to dissolution, that which hastens the end. . . . Witness *modern marriage*. It is obvious that all sense has gone out of modern marriage: which is, however, no objection to marriage but to modernity. The rationale of marriage lay in the legal sole responsibility of the man: marriage thereby had a centre of gravity, whereas now it limps with both legs. The rationale of marriage lay in its indissolubility in principle: it thereby acquired an accent which could *make itself heard* against the accidents of feeling, passion and the moment. It lay likewise in the responsibility of the families for the selection of mates. With the increasing indulgence of *love* matches one has simply eliminated the foundation of marriage, that alone which *makes* it an institution. One never establishes an institution on the basis of an idiosyncrasy, one does *not*, as aforesaid, establish marriage on the basis of 'love' – one establishes it on the basis of the sexual drive, the drive to own property (wife and child considered as property), the *drive to dominate* which continually organizes the smallest type of domain, the family, which *needs* children and heirs so as to retain, in a physiological sense as well, an achieved measure of power, influence, wealth, so as to prepare for protracted tasks, for a solidarity of instinct between the centuries. Marriage as an institution already includes in itself the affirmation of the largest, the most enduring form of organization: if society as a whole cannot *stand security* for itself to the most distant generations, then marriage has really no meaning. – Modern marriage has *lost* its meaning – consequently it is being abolished.

40

The labour question. – The stupidity, fundamentally the instinct degeneration which is the cause of *every* stupidity today, lies in the existence of a labour question at all. About certain things *one does not ask questions*: first imperative of instinct. – I simply cannot see what one wishes to do with the European worker now one has made a question of him. He finds himself far too well placed not to go on asking for more, or to ask more and more impudently. After all, he has the great majority on his side. There is absolutely no hope left that a modest and self-sufficient kind of human being, a type of Chinaman, should here form itself into a class: and this would have been sensible, this was actually a necessity. What has one done? – Everything designed to nip in the bud even the prerequisites for it – through the most irresponsible thoughtlessness one has totally destroyed the instincts by virtue of which the worker becomes possible as a class, possible *for himself*. The worker has been made liable for military service, he has been allowed to form unions and to vote: no wonder the worker already feels his existence to be a state of distress (expressed in moral terms as a state of *injustice*). But what does one *want*? – to ask it again. If one wills an end, one must also will the means to it: if one wants slaves, one is a fool if one educates them to be masters. –

41

'Freedom as I *do not* mean it.* . . .' – In times like these, to have to rely on one's instincts is one fatality more. These instincts contradict, disturb and destroy one another; I have already defined the *modern* as physiological self-contradiction. The rationale of education would seem to require that at least one of these instinct-systems should be *paralysed* beneath an iron pressure, so as to permit another to come into force, become strong, become master. Today the only way of making the individual possible would be by *pruning* him: possible,

* Alludes to Max von Schenkendorf's poem 'Freiheit, die ich meine' (Freedom as I mean it).

that is to say *complete*. . . . The reverse is what actually happens: the claim to independence, to free development, to *laisser aller*, is advanced most heatedly by precisely those for whom no curb *could be too strong* – this applies *in politicis*, it applies in art. But this is a symptom of *décadence*: our modern concept 'freedom' is one more proof of degeneration of instinct. –

42

Where faith is needed. – Nothing is rarer among moralists and saints than integrity; perhaps they say the opposite, perhaps they even *believe* it. For when faith is more useful, effective, convincing than *conscious* hypocrisy, hypocrisy instinctively and forthwith becomes *innocent*: first principle for the understanding of great saints. In the case of philosophers too, a different kind of saint, their entire trade demands that they concede only certain truths: namely those through which their trade receives *public* sanction – in Kantian terms, truths of *practical* reason. They know what they *have* to prove, they are practical in that – they recognize one another by their agreement over 'truths'. – 'Thou shalt not lie' – in plain words: *take care*, philosopher, not to tell the truth . . .

43

In the ear of the Conservatives. – What was formerly not known, what is known today or could be known – a *reversion*, a turning back in any sense and to any degree, is quite impossible. We physiologists at least know that. But all priests and moralists have believed it was possible – they have *wanted* to take mankind back, *force* it back, to an *earlier* standard of virtue. Morality has always been a bed of Procrustes. Even politicians have in this matter imitated the preachers of virtue: even today there are parties whose goal is a dream of the crabwise *retrogression* of all things. But no one is free to be a crab. There is nothing for it: one *has* to go forward, which is to say *step by step further into décadence* (– this is *my* definition of modern 'progress' . . .). One can *retard* this development and, through retardation, dam and gather up degeneration itself and make it more vehement and *sudden*: more one cannot do. –

44

My conception of the genius. – Great men, like great epochs, are explosive material in whom tremendous energy has been accumulated; their prerequisite has always been, historically and physiologically, that a protracted assembling, accumulating, economizing and preserving has preceded them – that there has been no explosion for a long time. If the tension in the mass has grown too great the merest accidental stimulus suffices to call the 'genius', the 'deed', the great destiny, into the world. Of what account then are circumstances, the epoch, the *Zeitgeist*, public opinion! – Take the case of Napoleon. The France of the Revolution, and even more pre-Revolution France, would have brought forth the type antithetical to Napoleon: it *did* bring it forth, moreover. And because Napoleon was *different*, the heir of a stronger, longer, older civilization than that which was going up in dust and smoke in France, he became master here, he alone *was* master here. Great human beings are necessary, the epoch in which they appear is accidental; that they almost always become master of their epoch is only because they are stronger, because they are older, because a longer assembling of force has preceded them. The relationship between a genius and his epoch is the same as that between strong and weak, and as that between old and young: the epoch is always relatively much younger, less substantial, more immature, less sure of itself, more childish. – That they have *very different* ideas on this subject in France today (in Germany too, but that is of no consequence), that there the theory of milieu, a real neurotic's theory, has become sacrosanct and almost scientific and finds credence even among physiologists – that fact has an 'ill odour' and gives one sadly to think. – The same ideas are believed in England too, but no one will lose any sleep over that. The Englishman has only two possible ways of coming to terms with the genius and 'great man': either the *democratic* way in the manner of

Buckle or the *religious* way in the manner of Carlyle. – The *danger* which lies in great human beings and great epochs is extraordinary; sterility, exhaustion of every kind follow in their footsteps. The great human being is a terminus; the great epoch, the Renaissance for example, is a terminus. The genius – in his works, in his deeds – is necessarily a prodigal: his greatness lies in the fact that *he expends himself*. . . . The instinct of self-preservation is as it were suspended; the overwhelming pressure of the energies which emanate from him forbids him any such care and prudence. One calls this 'sacrifice'; one praises his 'heroism' therein, his indifference to his own interests, his devotion to an idea, a great cause, a fatherland: all misunderstandings. . . . He flows out, he overflows, he uses himself up, he does not spare himself – with inevitability, fatefully, involuntarily, as a river's bursting its banks is involuntary. But because one owes a great deal to such explosive beings one has bestowed a great deal upon them in return, for example a species of *higher morality*. . . . For that is the nature of human gratitude: it *misunderstands* its benefactors. –

45

The criminal and what is related to him. – The criminal type is the type of the strong human being under unfavourable conditions, a strong human being made sick. What he lacks is the wilderness, a certain freer and more perilous nature and form of existence in which all that is attack and defence in the instinct of the strong human being *comes into its own*. His *virtues* have been excommunicated by society; the liveliest drives within him forthwith blend with the depressive emotions, with suspicion, fear, dishonour. But this is almost the *recipe* for physiological degeneration. He who has to do in secret what he does best and most likes to do, with protracted tension, caution, slyness, becomes anaemic; and because he has never harvested anything from his instincts but danger, persecution, disaster, his feelings too turn against these instincts – he feels them to be a fatality. It is society, our tame, mediocre, gelded society, in which a human being raised in nature, who comes from the mountains or from adventures of the sea, necessarily degenerates into a criminal. Or almost necessarily: for there are cases in which such a human being proves stronger than society: the Corsican Napoleon is the most famous case. In regard to the problem before us the testimony of Dostoyevsky is of importance – Dostoyevsky, the only psychologist, by the way, from whom I had anything to learn: he is one of the happiest accidents of my life, even more so than my discovery of Stendhal. This *profound* human being, who was ten times justified in despising the superficial Germans, found the Siberian convicts in whose midst he lived for a long time, nothing but the worst criminals for whom no return to society was possible, very different from what he himself had expected – he found them to be carved out of about the best, hardest and most valuable timber growing anywhere on Russian soil. Let us generalize the case of the criminal: let us think of natures which, for whatever reason, lack public approval, which know they are not considered beneficial or useful, that Chandala feeling that one is considered not an equal but as thrust out, as unworthy, as a source of pollution. The colour of the subterranean is on the thoughts and actions of such natures; everything in them becomes paler than in those upon whose existence the light of day reposes. But virtually every form of existence which we treat with distinction today formerly lived in this semi-gravelike atmosphere: the scientific nature, the artist, the genius, the free spirit, the actor, the merchant, the great discoverer. . . . As long as the *priest* was considered the highest type *every* valuable kind of human being was disvalued. . . . The time is coming – I promise it – when he will be considered the *lowest*, as *our* Chandala, as the most mendacious, as the most indecent kind of human being. . . . I draw attention to the fact that even now, under the mildest rule of custom which has ever obtained on earth or at any rate in Europe, every kind of apartness, every protracted, all too protracted *keeping under*, every uncommon, untransparent form of existence, brings men close to that type of which the criminal is the perfection. All innovators of the spirit bear for a time the pallid, fatalistic sign of the

Chandala on their brow: *not* because they are felt to be so, but because they themselves feel the terrible chasm which divides them from all that is traditional and held in honour. Almost every genius knows as one of the phases of his development the 'Catilinarian existence', a feeling of hatred, revengefulness and revolt against everything which already *is*, which is no longer *becoming*. . . . Catiline – the antecedent form of *every* Caesar. –

46

*Here is the prospect free.** – When a philosopher keeps silent, it can be loftiness of soul; when he contradicts himself, it can be love; a politeness which tells lies is possible in men of knowledge. Not without subtlety was it said: *il est indigne des grands coeurs de répandre le trouble qu'ils ressentent*:† only one has to add that not to fear *the unworthiest things* can likewise be greatness of soul. A woman who loves sacrifices her honour; a man of knowledge who 'loves' sacrifices perhaps his humanity; a god who loved became a Jew . . .

47

Beauty no accident. – Even the beauty of a race or a family, the charm and benevolence of their whole demeanour, is earned by labour: like genius, it is the final result of the accumulatory labour of generations. One must have made great sacrifices to good taste, one must for its sake have done many things, left many things undone – the French seventeenth century is admirable in both – one must have possessed in it a selective principle in respect of one's society, residence, dress, sexual gratification, one must have preferred beauty to advantage, habit, opinion, indolence. Supreme rule of conduct: even when alone one must not 'let oneself go'. – Good things are costly beyond measure: and the law still holds that he who *has* them is different from him who *obtains* them. Everything good is

* Quotation from the closing scene of *Faust,* Part Two.
† It is unworthy of great spirits to spread abroad the agitation they feel.

inheritance: what is not inherited is imperfect, is a beginning.
. . . In Athens at the time of Cicero, who expressed his surprise
at it, the men and youths were of far superior beauty to the
women: but what labour and exertion in the service of beauty
the male sex of that place had for centuries demanded of themselves! – For one must not mistake the method involved here:
a mere disciplining of thoughts and feelings is virtually nothing (– here lies the great mistake of German culture, which is
totally illusory): one first has to convince the *body*. The strict
maintenance of a significant and select demeanour, an obliga-
tion to live only among men who do not 'let themselves go',
completely suffices for becoming significant and select: in two
or three generations everything is already *internalized*. It is
decisive for the fortune of nations and of mankind that one
should inaugurate culture in the *right place* – *not* in the 'soul' (as
has been the fateful superstition of priests and quasi-priests):
the right place is the body, demeanour, diet, physiology: the
rest follows. . . . This is why the Greeks remain the *supreme
cultural event* of history – they knew, they *did* what needed to be
done; Christianity, which despised the body, has up till now
been mankind's greatest misfortune. –

48

Progress in my sense. – I too speak of a 'return to nature',
although it is not really a going-back but a *going-up* – up into a
high, free, even frightful nature and naturalness, such as plays
with great tasks, is *permitted* to play with them. . . . To speak in
a *parable*: Napoleon was a piece of 'return to nature' as I
understand it (for example *in rebus tacticis*,* even more, as
military men know, in strategy). – But Rousseau – where did
he really want to return to? Rousseau, this first modern man,
idealist and *canaille* in *one* person; who needed moral 'dignity'
in order to endure his own aspect; sick with unbridled vanity
and unbridled self-contempt. Even this abortion recumbent
on the threshold of the new age wanted a 'return to nature' –
where, to ask it again, did Rousseau want to return to? – I

* in respect of tactics.

hate Rousseau even *in* the Revolution: it is the world-historical expression of this duplicity of idealist and *canaille*. The bloody farce enacted by this Revolution, its 'immorality', does not concern me much: what I hate is its Rousseauesque *morality* – the so-called 'truths' of the Revolution through which it is still an active force and persuades everything shallow and mediocre over to its side. The doctrine of equality! ... But there exists no more poisonous poison: for it *seems* to be preached by justice itself, while it is the *end* of justice. ... 'Equality for equals, inequality for unequals' – *that* would be the true voice of justice: and, what follows from it, 'Never make equal what is unequal'. – That such dreadful and bloody happenings have surrounded this doctrine of equality has given this 'modern idea' *par excellence* a kind of glory and lurid glow, so that the Revolution as a *spectacle* has seduced even the noblest spirits. That is, however, no reason for esteeming it any more highly. – I see only one who experienced it as it has to be experienced – with *disgust* – Goethe ...

49

Goethe – not a German event but a European one: a grand attempt to overcome the eighteenth century through a return to nature, through a going-*up* to the naturalness of the Renaissance, a kind of self-overcoming on the part of that century. – He bore within him its strongest instincts: sentimentality, nature-idolatry, the anti-historical, the idealistic, the unreal and revolutionary (– the last is only a form of the unreal). He called to his aid history, the natural sciences, antiquity, likewise Spinoza, above all practical activity; he surrounded himself with nothing but closed horizons; he did not sever himself from life, he placed himself within it; nothing could discourage him and he took as much as possible upon himself, above himself, within himself. What he aspired to was *totality*; he strove against the separation of reason, sensuality, feeling, will (– preached in the most horrible scholasticism by Kant, the antipodes of Goethe); he disciplined himself to a whole, he *created* himself. ... Goethe was, in an epoch disposed to the unreal, a convinced realist: he affirmed everything which was related to him in this respect—he had no greater experience than that *ens realissimum* called Napoleon. Goethe conceived of a strong, highly cultured human being, skilled in all physical accomplishments, who, keeping himself in check and having reverence for himself, dares to allow himself the whole compass and wealth of naturalness, who is strong enough for this freedom; a man of tolerance, not out of weakness, but out of strength, because he knows how to employ to his advantage what would destroy an average nature; a man to whom nothing is forbidden, except it be *weakness*, whether that weakness be called vice or virtue. . . . A spirit thus *emancipated* stands in the midst of the universe with a joyful and trusting fatalism, in the *faith* that only what is separate and individual may be rejected, that in the totality everything is redeemed and affirmed – *he no longer denies*. . . . But such a faith is the highest of all possible faiths: I have baptised it with the name *Dionysus*.* –

50

One could say that in a certain sense the nineteenth century has *also* striven for what Goethe as a person strove for: universality in understanding and affirmation, amenability to experience of whatever kind, reckless realism, reverence for everything factual. How does it happen that the total result is not a Goethe but a chaos, a nihilistic sigh, a not knowing which way to turn, an instinct of weariness which *in praxi* continually tries *to reach back to the eighteenth century*? (– for example as romanticism of feeling, as altruism and hypersentimentality, as feminism in taste, as Socialism in politics). Is the nineteenth century, especially in its closing decades, not merely a strengthened, *brutalized* eighteenth century, that is to say a century of *décadence*? So that Goethe would have been, not merely for Germany but for all Europe, merely an episode, a beautiful 'in vain'? – But one misunderstands great human beings if one views them from the paltry perspective of public

* For a note on Dionysus, see Appendix H.

utility. That one does not know how to make any use of it *perhaps even pertains* to greatness ...

51

Goethe is the last German before whom I feel reverence: he would have felt three things which I feel – we are also in agreement over the 'Cross'.* ... I am often asked why it is I write in *German*: nowhere am I worse read than in the Fatherland. But who knows, after all, whether I even *wish* to be read today? – To create things upon which time tries its teeth in vain; in form and in *substance* to strive after a little immortality – I have never been modest enough to demand less of myself. The aphorism, the apophthegm, in which I am the first master among Germans, are the forms of 'eternity'; my ambition is to say in ten sentences what everyone else says in a book – what everyone else *does not* say in a book... I have given mankind the profoundest book it possesses, my *Zarathustra*: I shall shortly give it the most independent.† –

* Refers to Goethe's *Venetian Epigrams,* in which the Cross is one of four things Goethe says he cannot endure.

† i.e. the *Revaluation of all Values.*

What I Owe to the Ancients

I

In conclusion, a word on that world into which I have sought to find a way, into which I have perhaps found a new way – the ancient world. My taste, which may be called the opposite of a tolerant taste, is even here far from uttering a wholesale Yes: in general it dislikes saying Yes, it would rather say No, most of all it prefers to say nothing at all. . . . This applies to entire cultures, it applies to books – it also applies to towns and countrysides. It is really only quite a small number of books of antiquity which count for anything in my life; the most famous are not among them. My sense of style, of the epigram as style, was awoken almost instantaneously on coming into contact with Sallust. I have not forgotten the astonishment of my honoured teacher Corssen when he had to give top marks to his worst Latin scholar – I had done all in a single blow. Compact, severe, with as much substance as possible, a cold malice towards 'fine words', also towards 'fine feelings' – in that I knew myself. One will recognize in my writings, even in my *Zarathustra*, a very serious ambition for *Roman* style, for the '*aera perennius*'* in style. – I had the same experience on first coming into contact with Horace. From that day to this no poet has given me the same artistic delight as I derived from the very first from an Horatian ode. In certain languages what is achieved here is not even *desirable*. This mosaic of words in which every word, as sound, as locus, as concept, pours forth its power to left and right and over the whole, this minimum in the range and number of signs which achieves a maximum of energy of these signs – all this is Roman and, if one will believe me, *noble par excellence*. All other poetry becomes by comparison somewhat too popular – a mere emotional garrulousness . . .

* more enduring than brass.

2

I received absolutely no such strong impressions from the Greeks; and, not to mince words, they *cannot* be to us what the Romans are. One does not *learn* from the Greeks – their manner is too strange, it is also too fluid to produce an imperative, a 'classical' effect. Who would ever have learned to write from a Greek! Who would ever have learned it *without* the Romans! . . . Let no one offer me Plato as an objection. In respect to Plato I am a thorough sceptic and have always been unable to join in the admiration of Plato the *artist* which is traditional among scholars. After all, I have here the most refined judges of taste of antiquity themselves on my side. It seems to me that Plato mixes together all forms of style; he is therewith in the matter of style a *first décadent*: he has on his conscience something similar to the Cynics who devised the *Satura Menippea*.* For the Platonic dialogue, that frightfully self-satisfied and childish kind of dialectics, to operate as a stimulus one must never have read any good French writers – Fontenelle, for example. Plato is boring. – Ultimately my mistrust of Plato extends to the very bottom of him: I find him deviated so far from all the fundamental instincts of the Hellenes, so morally infected, so much an antecedent Christian – he already has the concept 'good' as the supreme concept – that I should prefer to describe the entire phenomenon 'Plato' by the harsh term 'higher swindle' or, if you prefer, 'idealism', than by any other. It has cost us dear that this Athenian went to school with the Egyptians (– or with the Jews in Egypt? . . .). In the great fatality of Christianity, Plato is that ambiguity and fascination called the 'ideal' which made it possible for the nobler natures of antiquity to misunderstand themselves and to step on to the *bridge* which led to the 'Cross'. . . . And how much there still is of Plato in the concept 'Church', in the structure, system, practice of the Church! – My recreation, my preference, my *cure* from all Platonism has always been *Thucydides*. Thucydides, and perhaps the *Principe* of Machia-

---

* Menippus (third century B.C.), of the Cynic school of philosophy, produced a number of satires no longer extant.

velli, are related to me closely by their unconditional will not to deceive themselves and to see reason in *reality* – not in 'reason', still less in 'morality'. .... For the deplorable embellishment of the Greeks with the colours of the ideal which the 'classically educated' youth carries away with him into life as the reward of his grammar-school drilling there is no more radical cure than Thucydides. One must turn him over line by line and read his hidden thoughts as clearly as his words: there are few thinkers so rich in hidden thoughts. *Sophist culture*, by which I mean *realist culture*, attains in him its perfect expression – this invaluable movement in the midst of the morality-and-ideal swindle of the Socratic schools which was then breaking out everywhere. Greek philosophy as the *décadence* of the Greek instinct; Thucydides as the grand summation, the last manifestation of that strong, stern, hard matter-of-factness instinctive to the older Hellenes. *Courage* in face of reality ultimately distinguishes such natures as Thucydides and Plato: Plato is a coward in face of reality – consequently he flees into the ideal; Thucydides has *himself* under control – consequently he retains control over things ...

3

From scenting out 'beautiful souls',* 'golden means' and other perfections in the Greeks, from admiring in them such things as their repose in grandeur, their ideal disposition, their sublime simplicity – from this 'sublime simplicity', a *niaiserie allemande*† when all is said and done, I was preserved by the psychologist in me. I saw their strongest instinct, the will to power, I saw them trembling at the intractable force of this drive – I saw all their institutions evolve out of protective measures designed for mutual security against the *explosive material* within them. The tremendous internal tension then discharged itself in fearful and ruthless external hostility: the

---

* From the title of Book VII of Goethe's novel *Wilhelm Meister's Apprenticeship:* 'Confessions of a Beautiful Soul'.
† German foolishness.

city states tore one another to pieces so that the citizens of each of them might find peace within himself. One needed to be strong: danger was close at hand – it lurked everywhere. The splendid supple physique, the reckless realism and immoralism which pertains to the Hellene was a *necessity*, not a 'natural quality'. It was produced, it was not there from the beginning. And one employed festivals and arts for no other purpose than to feel oneself *dominant*, to *show* oneself dominant: they are means for making oneself feared. . . . To judge the Greeks by their philosophers, in the German manner, perchance to employ the philistinism of the Socratic schools as a clue to what is fundamentally Hellenic! . . . But the philosophers are the *décadents* of Hellenism, the counter-movement against the old, the noble taste (– against the agonal instinct, against the *polis*, against the value of the race, against the authority of tradition). The Socratic virtues were preached *because* the Greeks had lost them: excitable, timid, fickle, comedians every one, they had more than enough reason to let morality be preached to them. Not that it would have done any good: but big words and fine attitudes are so suited to *décadents* . . .

4

I was the first to take seriously that wonderful phenomenon which bears the name Dionysus as a means to understanding the older Hellenic instinct, an instinct still exuberant and even overflowing: it is explicable only as an *excess* of energy. Whoever has investigated the Greeks, such as that profoundest student of their culture now living, Jacob Burckhardt of Basel, realizes at once the value of this line of approach: Burckhardt inserted a special section on the said phenomenon into his *Culture of the Greeks*. For the opposite of this, one should take a look at the almost laughable poverty of instinct displayed by German philologists whenever they approach the Dionysian. The celebrated Lobeck especially, who crept into this world of mysterious states with the honest self-confidence of a dried-up bookworm and by being nauseously frivolous and childish persuaded himself he was being scientific –

Lobeck intimated, with a great display of erudition, that these curiosities were of no consequence. To be sure, the priests might have communicated a number of valuable pieces of information to the participants in such orgies – that wine arouses desire, for example, that man can live on fruit if need be, that plants bloom in spring and wither in autumn. As regards that strange wealth of rites, symbols and myths of orgiastic origin with which the antique world was quite literally overrun, Lobeck finds in them an occasion for becoming a trifle more ingenious. 'When the Greeks had nothing else to do,' he says (*Aglaophamus* I, 672), 'they used to laugh, jump, race about, or, since man sometimes feels a desire for this, they used to sit down and weep and wail. *Others* later came along and sought some reason for this striking behaviour; and thus those countless myths and legends arose to explain these practices. On the other hand, one believed that the *droll activities* which now took place on festival days necessarily pertained to festival celebration and retained them as an indispensable part of divine worship.' – This is contemptible chatter and no one is likely to take a Lobeck seriously for a moment. We are affected quite differently when we probe the concept 'Greek' which Winckelmann and Goethe constructed for themselves and find it incompatible with that element out of which Dionysian art evolved – the orgy. I have, in fact, no doubt that Goethe would have utterly excluded anything of this kind from the possibilities of the Greek soul. *Consequently Goethe did not understand the Greeks.* For it is only in the Dionysian mysteries, in the psychology of the Dionysian condition, that the *fundamental fact* of the Hellenic instinct expresses itself – its 'will to life'. *What* did the Hellene guarantee to himself with these mysteries? *Eternal* life, the eternal recurrence of life; the future promised and consecrated in the past; the triumphant Yes to life beyond death and change; *true* life as collective continuation of life through procreation, through the mysteries of sexuality. It was for this reason that the *sexual* symbol was to the Greeks the symbol venerable as such, the intrinsic profound meaning of all antique piety. Every individual detail in the act of procreation, pregnancy, birth, awoke the most exalted and solemn feelings. In the teachings of the mysteries, *pain* is sanctified: the 'pains of childbirth' sanctify pain in general – all becoming and growing, all that guarantees the future, *postulates* pain. . . . For the eternal joy in creating to exist, for the will to life eternally to affirm itself, the 'torment of childbirth' *must* also exist eternally. . . . All this is contained in the word Dionysus: I know of no more exalted symbolism than this *Greek* symbolism, the symbolism of the Dionysian. The profoundest instinct of life, the instinct for the future of life, for the eternity of life, is in this word experienced religiously – the actual road to life, procreation, as the *sacred road*. . . . It was only Christianity, with *ressentiment against* life in its foundations, which made of sexuality something impure: it threw *filth* on the beginning, on the prerequisite of our life . . .

5

The psychology of the orgy as an overflowing feeling of life and energy within which even pain acts as a stimulus provided me with the key to the concept of the *tragic* feeling, which was misunderstood as much by Aristotle as it especially was by our pessimists. Tragedy is so far from providing evidence for pessimism among the Hellenes in Schopenhauer's sense that it has to be considered the decisive repudiation of that idea and the *counter-verdict* to it. Affirmation of life even in its strangest and sternest problems, the will to life rejoicing in its own inexhaustibility through the *sacrifice* of its highest types – *that* is what I called Dionysian, *that* is what I recognized as the bridge to the psychology of the *tragic* poet. *Not* so as to get rid of pity and terror, not so as to purify oneself of a dangerous emotion through its vehement discharge – it was thus Aristotle understood it – : but, beyond pity and terror, *to realize in oneself* the eternal joy of becoming – that joy which also encompasses *joy in destruction*. . . . And with that I again return to the place from which I set out – the *Birth of Tragedy* was my first revaluation of all values: with that I again plant myself in the soil out of which I draw all that I will and *can* – I, the last disciple of the philosopher Dionysus – I, the teacher of the eternal recurrence . . .*

* For Nietzsche's theory that all events recur eternally and its emotional significance in providing the most extreme formula of life-affirmation, see *Thus Spoke Zarathustra,* Part III ('Of the Vision and the Riddle', 'The Convalescent' and 'The Seven Seals') and Part IV ('The Intoxicated Song').

The Hammer Speaks

'*Why so hard?*' *the charcoal once said to the diamond;* '*for are we not close relations?*'

Why so soft? O my brothers, thus I ask you: for are you not – my brothers?

Why so soft, unresisting and yielding? Why is there so much denial and abnegation in your hearts? So little fate in your glances?

And if you will not be fates, if you will not be inexorable: how can you – conquer with me?

And if your hardness will not flash and cut and cut to pieces: how can you one day – create with me?

For all creators are hard. And it must seem bliss to you to press your hand upon millennia as upon wax,

bliss to write upon the will of millennia as upon metal – harder than metal, nobler than metal. Only the noblest is perfectly hard.

*This new law-table do I put over you, O my brothers: Become hard!**

* From *Thus Spoke Zarathustra*, Part III, 'Of Old and New Law-Tables', with minor variants.

THE ANTI-CHRIST

Foreword

THIS book belongs to the very few. Perhaps none of them is even living yet. Possibly they are the readers who understand my *Zarathustra*: how *could* I confound myself with those for whom there are ears listening today? – Only the day after tomorrow belongs to me. Some are born posthumously.

The conditions under which one understands me and then *necessarily* understands – I know them all too well. One must be honest in intellectual matters to the point of harshness to so much as endure my seriousness, my passion. One must be accustomed to living on mountains – to seeing the wretched ephemeral chatter of politics and national egoism *beneath* one. One must have become indifferent, one must never ask whether truth is useful or a fatality.... Strength which prefers questions for which no one today is sufficiently daring; courage for the *forbidden*; predestination for the labyrinth. An experience out of seven solitudes. New ears for new music. New eyes for the most distant things. A new conscience for truths which have hitherto remained dumb. *And* the will to economy in the grand style: to keeping one's energy, one's *enthusiasm* in bounds.... Reverence for oneself; love for oneself; unconditional freedom with respect to oneself ...

Very well! These alone are my readers, my rightful readers, my predestined readers: what do the *rest* matter? – The rest are merely mankind. – One must be superior to mankind in force, in *loftiness* of soul – in contempt ...

Friedrich Nietzsche

– Let us look one another in the face. We are Hyperboreans* –
we know well enough how much out of the way we live.
'Neither by land nor by sea shalt thou find the road to the
Hyperboreans': Pindar already knew that of us. Beyond the
North, beyond the ice, beyond death – *our* life, *our* happiness.
... We have discovered happiness, we know the road, we
have found the exit out of whole millennia of labyrinth. Who
else has found it? – Modern man perhaps? – 'I know not
which way to turn; I am everything that knows not which
way to turn' – sighs modern man. ... It was from *this* modernity that we were ill – from lazy peace, from cowardly
compromise, from the whole virtuous uncleanliness of modern
Yes and No. This tolerance and *largeur* of heart which 'forgives' everything because it 'understands' everything is
sirocco to us. Better to live among ice than among modern
virtues and other south winds! ... We were brave enough,
we spared neither ourselves nor others: but for long we did
not know *where* to apply our courage. We became gloomy, we
were called fatalists. *Our* fatality – was the plenitude, the
tension, the blocking-up of our forces. We thirsted for lightning and action, of all things we kept ourselves furthest from
the happiness of the weaklings, from 'resignation'. ... There
was a thunderstorm in our air, the nature which we are grew
dark – *for we had no road*. Formula of our happiness: a Yes, a
No, a straight line, a *goal* ...

2

What is good? – All that heightens the feeling of power, the
will to power, power itself in man.

What is bad? – All that proceeds from weakness.

What is happiness? – The feeling that power *increases* – that
a resistance is overcome.

* In Greek mythology a race dwelling beyond the north wind (Boreas)
in a country of warmth and plenty.

Not contentment, but more power; *not* peace at all, but war; *not* virtue, but proficiency (virtue in the Renaissance style, *virtù*, virtue free of moralic acid).

The weak and ill-constituted shall perish: first principle of *our* philanthropy. And one shall help them to do so.

What is more harmful than any vice? – Active sympathy for the ill-constituted and weak – Christianity . . .

3

The problem I raise here is not what ought to succeed mankind in the sequence of species (– the human being is an *end* –): but what type of human being one ought to *breed*, ought to *will*, as more valuable, more worthy of life, more certain of the future.

This more valuable type has existed often enough already: but as a lucky accident, as an exception, never as *willed*. *He* has rather been the most feared, he has hitherto been virtually *the* thing to be feared – and out of fear the reverse type has been willed, bred, *achieved*: the domestic animal, the herd animal, the sick animal man – the Christian . . .

4

Mankind does *not* represent a development of the better or the stronger or the higher in the way that is believed today. 'Progress' is merely a modern idea, that is to say a false idea. The European of today is of far less value than the European of the Renaissance; onward development is not by *any* means, by any necessity the same thing as elevation, advance, strengthening.

In another sense there are cases of individual success constantly appearing in the most various parts of the earth and from the most various cultures in which a *higher type* does manifest itself: something which in relation to collective mankind is a sort of superman. Such chance occurrences of great success have always been possible and perhaps always will be possible. And even entire races, tribes, nations can under certain circumstances represent such a *lucky hit*.

5

One should not embellish or dress up Christianity: it has waged a *war to the death* against this *higher* type of man, it has excommunicated all the fundamental instincts of this type, it has distilled evil, the *Evil One*, out of these instincts – the strong human being as the type of reprehensibility, as the 'outcast'. Christianity has taken the side of everything weak, base, ill-constituted, it has made an ideal out of *opposition* to the preservative instincts of strong life; it has depraved the reason even of the intellectually strongest natures by teaching men to feel the supreme values of intellectuality as sinful, as misleading, as *temptations*. The most deplorable example: the depraving of Pascal, who believed his reason had been depraved by original sin while it had only been depraved by his Christianity! –

6

It is a painful, a dreadful spectacle which has opened up before me: I have drawn back the curtain on the *depravity* of man. In my mouth this word is protected against at any rate one suspicion: that it contains a moral accusation of man. It is – I should like to underline the fact again – free of any *moralic acid*: and this to the extent that I find that depravity precisely where hitherto one most consciously aspired to 'virtue', to 'divinity'. I understand depravity, as will already have been guessed, in the sense of *décadence*: my assertion is that all the values in which mankind at present summarizes its highest desideratum are *décadence values*.

I call an animal, a species, an individual depraved when it loses its instincts, when it chooses, when it *prefers* what is harmful to it. A history of the 'higher feelings', of the 'ideals of mankind' – and it is possible I shall have to narrate it – would almost also constitute an explanation of *why* man is so depraved. I consider life itself instinct for growth, for continuence, for accumulation of forces, for *power*: where the will to power is lacking there is decline. My assertion is that this will is *lacking* in all the supreme values of mankind – that values of decline, *nihilistic* values hold sway under the holiest names.

7

Christianity is called the religion of *pity*. – Pity stands in antithesis to the tonic emotions which enhance the energy of the feeling of life: it has a depressive effect. One loses force when one pities. The loss of force which life has already sustained through suffering is increased and multiplied even further by pity. Suffering itself becomes contagious through pity; sometimes it can bring about a collective loss of life and life-energy which stands in an absurd relation to the quantum of its cause (– the case of the death of the Nazarene). This is the first aspect; but there is an even more important one. If one judges pity by the value of the reactions which it usually brings about, its mortally dangerous character appears in a much clearer light. Pity on the whole thwarts the law of evolution, which is the law of *selection*. It preserves what is ripe for destruction; it defends life's disinherited and condemned; through the abundance of the ill-constituted of all kinds which it *retains* in life it gives life itself a gloomy and questionable aspect. One has ventured to call pity a virtue (– in every *noble* morality it counts as weakness –); one has gone further, one has made of it *the* virtue, the ground and origin of all virtue – only, to be sure, from the viewpoint of a nihilistic philosophy which inscribed *Denial of Life* on its escutcheon – a fact always to be kept in view. Schopenhauer was within his rights in this: life is denied, made *more worthy of denial* by pity – pity is *practical* nihilism. To say it again, this depressive and contagious instinct thwarts those instincts bent on preserving and enhancing the value of life: both as a *multiplier* of misery and as a *conservator* of everything miserable it is one of the chief instruments for the advancement of *décadence* – pity persuades to *nothingness*! ... One does not say 'nothingness': one says 'the Beyond'; or 'God'; or '*true* life'; or Nirvana, redemption, blessedness. ... This innocent rhetoric from the domain of religio-moral idiosyncrasy at once appears *much less innocent* when one grasps *which* tendency is here draping the mantle of sublime words about itself: the tendency *hostile to life*. Schopenhauer was hostile to life: *therefore* pity became for him a virtue. ... Aristotle, as is well known, saw in pity a morbid and dangerous condition which one did well to get at from time to time with a purgative: he understood tragedy as a purgative. From the instinct for life one would indeed have to seek some means of puncturing so morbid and dangerous an accumulation of pity as that represented by the case of Schopenhauer (and unfortunately also by our entire literary and artistic *décadence* from St Petersburg to Paris, from Tolstoy to Wagner), so that it might *burst*. ... Nothing in our unhealthy modernity is more unhealthy than Christian pity. To be physician *here*, to be inexorable *here*, to wield the knife *here* – that pertains to *us*, that is *our* kind of philanthropy, with that are *we* philosophers, we Hyperboreans! –

8

It is necessary to say *whom* we feel to be our antithesis – the theologians and all that has theologian blood in its veins – our entire philosophy. ... One must have seen the fatality from close up, better still one must have experienced it in oneself, one must have almost perished by it, no longer to find anything funny here (the free-thinking of our naturalists and physiologists is to my mind *funny* – they lack passion in these things, they do not *suffer* from them –). That poison extends much further than one thinks: I have discovered the arrogant theologian-instinct wherever anyone today feels himself to be an 'idealist' – wherever anyone assumes, by virtue of a higher origin, a right to cast strange and superior looks at actuality. ... Just like the priest, the idealist has all the great concepts in his hand (– and not only in his hand!), he plays them out with a benevolent contempt against the 'understanding', the 'senses', 'honours', 'luxury', 'science', he sees these things as *beneath* him, as harmful and seductive forces above which 'the spirit' soars in pure self-sufficiency – as though humility, chastity, poverty, in a word *holiness*, had not hitherto done life unutterably more harm than any sort of

frightfulness or vice whatever. . . . Pure spirit is pure lie. . . .
So long as the priest, that denier, calumniator and poisoner of
life by *profession*, still counts as a *higher* kind of human being,
there can be no answer to the question: what *is* truth? One
has already stood truth on its head when the conscious advocate
of denial and nothingness counts as the representative of
'truth' . . .

9

I make war on this theologian instinct: I have found traces of
it everywhere. Whoever has theologian blood in his veins has
a wrong and dishonest attitude towards all things from the
very first. The pathos that develops out of this is called *faith*:
closing one's eyes with respect to oneself for good and all so as
not to suffer from the sight of incurable falsity. Out of this
erroneous perspective on all things one makes a morality, a
virtue, a holiness for oneself, one unites the good conscience
with seeing *falsely* – one demands that no *other* kind of perspective shall be accorded any value after one has rendered one's
own sacrosanct with the names 'God', 'redemption', 'eternity'. I have dug out the theologian instinct everywhere: it is
the most widespread, peculiarly *subterranean* form of falsity
that exists on earth. What a theologian feels to be true *must*
be false: this provides almost a criterion of truth. It is his
deepest instinct of self-preservation which forbids any part of
reality whatever to be held in esteem or even spoken of.
Wherever the influence of the theologian extends *value judgement* is stood on its head, the concepts 'true' and 'false' are
necessarily reversed: that which is most harmful to life is here
called 'true', that which enhances, intensifies, affirms, justifies
it and causes it to triumph is called 'false'. . . . If it happens
that, by way of the 'conscience' of princes (*or* of nations –),
theologians stretch out their hands after *power*, let us be in no
doubt *what* at bottom is taking place every time: the will to
the end, the *nihilistic* will wants power . . .

10

Among Germans one will understand immediately when I say that philosophy has been corrupted by theologian blood. The Protestant pastor is the grandfather of German philosophy, Protestantism itself is its *peccatum originale*.* Definition of Protestantism: the halfsided paralysis of Christianity – *and* of reason. ... One has only to say the words 'College of Tübingen'† to grasp *what* German philosophy is at bottom – a *cunning* theology. ... The Swabians are the best liars in Germany, they lie innocently. ... Why the rejoicing heard throughout the German academic world – three-quarters composed of the sons of pastors and teachers – at the appearance of *Kant*? Why the Germans' conviction, which still finds an echo even today, that with Kant things were taking a turn for the *better*? The theologian instinct in the German scholar divined *what* was henceforth possible once again. ... A secret path to the old ideal stood revealed, the concept 'real world', the concept of morality as the *essence* of the world (– these two most vicious errors in existence!) were once more, thanks to a crafty-sly scepticism, if not demonstrable yet no longer *refutable*. ... Reason, the *right* of reason does not extend so far. ... One had made of reality an 'appearance'; one had made a completely *fabricated* world, that of being, into reality. ... Kant's success is merely a theologian's success: German integrity was far from firm and Kant, like Luther, like Leibniz, was one more constraint upon it ...

11

A word against Kant as *moralist*. A virtue has to be *our* invention, *our* most personal defence and necessity: in any other sense it is merely a danger. What does not condition our life *harms* it: a virtue merely from a feeling of respect for the concept 'virtue', as Kant desired it, is harmful. 'Virtue', 'duty', 'good in itself', impersonal and universal – phantoms,

---

* original sin.
† A famous theological college in Swabia.

expressions of decline, of the final exhaustion of life, of Königs-
bergian Chinadom. The profoundest laws of preservation and
growth demand the reverse of this: that each one of us should
devise *his own* virtue, *his own* categorical imperative. A people
perishes if it mistakes *its own* duty for the concept of duty in
general. Nothing works more profound ruin than any 'impersonal' duty, any sacrifice to the Moloch of abstraction. –
Kant's categorical imperative* should have been felt as *mortally dangerous*! . . . The theologian instinct alone took it under
its protection! – An action compelled by the instinct of life has
in the joy of performing it the proof it is a *right* action: and
every nihilist with Christian-dogmatic bowels understands joy
as an *objection*. . . . What destroys more quickly than to work, to
think, to feel without inner necessity, without a deep personal
choice, without *joy*? as an automaton of 'duty'? It is virtually
a *recipe* for *décadence*, even for idiocy. . . . Kant became an idiot.
– And that was the contemporary of *Goethe*! This fatal spider
counted as the *German* philosopher – still does! I take care not
to say what I think of the Germans. . . . Did Kant not see in
the French Revolution the transition from the inorganic form
of the state to the *organic*? Did he not ask himself whether
there was an event which could be explained in no other way
than by a moral predisposition on the part of mankind, so that
with it the 'tendency of man to seek the good' would be
proved once and for all? Kant's answer: 'The Revolution is
that.' The erring instinct in all and everything, *anti-naturalness*
as instinct, German *décadence* as philosophy – *that is Kant!* –

12

I exclude a few sceptics, the decent type in the history of
philosophy: but the rest are ignorant of the first requirements
of intellectual integrity. These great visionaries and prodigies
behave one and all like little women – they consider 'fine
feelings' arguments, the 'heaving bosom' the bellows of

---

* 'Act as if the maxim of your action were to become through your will
a general natural law' is one of the definitions of the 'categorical imperative' in Kant's *Metaphysic of Morals*.

divinity, conviction the *criterion* of truth. Finally Kant, in his 'German' innocence, tried to give this form of corruption, this lack of intellectual conscience, a scientific colouring with the concept 'practical reason': he designed a reason specifically for the case in which one was supposed not to have to bother about reason, namely when morality, when the sublime demand 'thou shalt' makes itself heard. If one considers that the philosopher is, in virtually all nations, only the further development of the priestly type, one is no longer surprised to discover this heirloom of the priest, *self-deceptive fraudulence*. If one has sacred tasks, for example that of improving, saving, redeeming mankind – if one carries the divinity in one's bosom, is the mouthpiece of an other-world imperative, such a mission already places one outside all merely reasonable valuations – one *is* already sanctified by such a task, one is already the type of a higher order! ... What does a priest care about *science*! He is above it! – And the priest has hitherto *ruled*! – *He has determined* the concept 'true' and 'untrue'! ...

13

Let us not undervalue this: *we ourselves*, we free spirits, are already a 'revaluation of all values', an *incarnate* declaration of war and victory over all ancient conceptions of 'true' and 'untrue'. The most valuable insights are the last to be discovered; but the most valuable insights are *methods*. *All* the methods, *all* the prerequisites of our present-day scientificality have for millennia been the objects of the profoundest contempt: on their account one was excluded from associating with 'honest' men – one was considered an 'enemy of God', a despiser of truth, a man 'possessed'. As a practitioner of science one was Chandala. ... We have had the whole pathos of mankind against us – its conception of what truth *ought* to be, what the service of truth *ought* to be; every 'thou shalt' has hitherto been directed *against* us. ... Our objectives, our practices, our quiet, cautious, mistrustful manner – all this appeared utterly unworthy and contemptible to mankind. – In the end one might reasonably ask oneself whether it was not really an *aesthetic* taste which blinded mankind for so long: it desired a *picturesque* effect from truth, it desired especially that the man of knowledge should produce a powerful impression on the senses. It was our *modesty* which offended their taste the longest. . . . Oh, how well they divined that fact, those turkey-cocks of God –

14

We have learned better. We have become more modest in every respect. We no longer trace the origin of man in the 'spirit', in the 'divinity', we have placed him back among the animals. We consider him the strongest animal because he is the most cunning: his spirituality is a consequence of this. On the other hand, we guard ourselves against a vanity which would like to find expression even here: the vanity that man is the great secret objective of animal evolution. Man is absolutely not the crown of creation: every creature stands beside him at the same stage of perfection. . . . And even in asserting that we assert too much: man is, relatively speaking, the most unsuccessful animal, the sickliest, the one most dangerously strayed from its instincts – with all that, to be sure, the most *interesting*! – As regards the animals, Descartes was the first who, with a boldness worthy of reverence, ventured to think of the animal as a *machine*: our whole science of physiology is devoted to proving this proposition. Nor, logically, do we exclude man, as even Descartes did: our knowledge of man today is real knowledge precisely to the extent that it is knowledge of him as a machine. Formerly man was presented with 'free will' as a dowry from a higher order: today we have taken even will away from him, in the sense that will may no longer be understood as a faculty. The old word 'will' only serves to designate a resultant, a kind of individual reaction which necessarily follows a host of partly contradictory, partly congruous stimuli – the will no longer 'effects' anything, no longer 'moves' anything. . . . Formerly one saw in man's consciousness, in his 'spirit', the proof of his higher origin, his divinity; to make himself *perfect* man was advised to draw his senses back into himself in the manner of the tortoise, to cease to have any traffic with the earthly, to lay aside his mortal frame: then the chief part of him would remain behind, 'pure spirit'. We have thought better of this too: becoming-conscious, 'spirit', is to us precisely a symptom of a relative imperfection of the organism, as an attempting, fumbling, blundering, as a toiling in which an unnecessarily large amount of nervous energy is expended – we deny that anything can be made perfect so long as it is still made conscious. 'Pure spirit' is pure stupidity: if we deduct the nervous system and the senses, the 'mortal frame', *we miscalculate* – that's all! . . .

15

In Christianity neither morality nor religion come into contact with reality at any point. Nothing but imaginary *causes* ('God', 'soul', 'ego', 'spirit', 'free will' – or 'unfree will'): nothing but imaginary *effects* ('sin', 'redemption', 'grace', 'punishment', 'forgiveness of sins'). A traffic between imaginary *beings* ('God', 'spirits', 'souls'); an imaginary *natural* science (anthropocentric; complete lack of the concept of natural causes); an imaginary *psychology* (nothing but self-misunderstandings, interpretations of pleasant or unpleasant general feelings, for example the condition of the *nervus sympathicus*, with the aid of the sign-language of religio-moral idiosyncrasy – 'repentance', 'sting of conscience', 'temptation by the Devil', 'the proximity of God'); an imaginary *teleology* ('the kingdom of God', 'the Last Judgement', 'eternal life'). – This purely fictitious world is distinguished from the world of dreams, very much to its disadvantage, by the fact that the latter *mirrors* actuality, while the former falsifies, disvalues and denies actuality. Once the concept 'nature' had been devised as the concept antithetical to 'God', 'natural' had to be the word for 'reprehensible' – this entire fictional world has its roots in *hatred* of the natural (– actuality! –), it is the expression of a profound discontent with the actual. . . . *But that explains everything*. Who alone has reason to *lie himself out* of actuality? He who *suffers* from it. But to suffer from actuality means to be an abortive actuality. . . . The preponderance of feelings of displeasure over feelings of pleasure is the *cause* of a fictitious morality and religion: such a preponderance, however, provides the *formula* for *décadence* . . .

16

A critical examination of the *Christian concept of God* invites a similar conclusion. – A people which still believes in itself still also has its own God. In him it venerates the conditions through which it has prospered, its virtues – it projects its joy in itself, its feeling of power on to a being whom one can thank for them. He who is rich wants to bestow; a proud people needs a God in order to *sacrifice*. . . . Within the bounds of such presuppositions religion is a form of gratitude. One is grateful for oneself: for that one needs a God. – Such a God must be able to be both useful and harmful, both friend and foe – he is admired in good and bad alike. The *anti-natural* castration of a God into a God of the merely good would be totally undesirable here. One has as much need of the evil God as of the good God: for one does not owe one's existence to philanthropy or tolerance precisely. . . . Of what consequence would a God be who knew nothing of anger, revengefulness, envy, mockery, cunning, acts of violence? to whom even the rapturous *ardeurs* of victory and destruction were unknown? One would not understand such a God: why should one have him? – To be sure: when a people is perishing; when it feels its faith in the future, its hope of freedom vanish completely; when it becomes conscious that the most profitable thing of all is submissiveness and that the virtues of submissiveness are a condition of its survival, then its God *has* to alter too. He now becomes a dissembler, timid, modest, counsels 'peace of soul', no more hatred, forbearance, 'love' even towards friend and foe. He is continually moralizing, he creeps into the cave of every private virtue, becomes a God for everybody, becomes a private man, becomes a cosmopolitan. . . . Formerly he represented a people, the strength of a people, everything aggressive and thirsting for power in the soul of a people: now he is merely the good God. . . . There is in fact no other alternative for Gods: *either* they are the will to power – and so long as they are that they will be national Gods – *or* else the impotence for power – and then they necessarily become *good* . . .

17

Wherever the will to power declines in any form there is every time also a physiological regression, a *décadence*. The divinity of *décadence*, pruned of all its manliest drives and virtues, from now on necessarily becomes the God of the physiologically retarded, the weak. They do *not* call themselves the weak, they call themselves 'the good'. . . . One will understand without further indication at what moment of history the dual fiction of a good and an evil God first becomes possible. The same instinct which makes the subjugated people reduce its God to the 'good in itself' makes them expunge the good qualities from the God of their conqueror; they revenge themselves on their masters by changing their masters' God into a devil. – The *good* God and the Devil: both products of *décadence*. – How can one today still defer so far to the simplicity of Christian theologians as to join them in proclaiming that the evolution of the concept of God from the 'God of Israel', the national God, to the Christian God, the epitome of everything good, is an *advance*? – But even Renan does so. As if Renan had a right to simplicity! For it is the opposite which leaps to the eye. When the prerequisites of *ascending* life, when everything strong, brave, masterful, proud is eliminated from the concept of God; when he declines step by step to the symbol of a staff for the weary, a sheet-anchor for all who are drowning; when he becomes the poor people's God, the sinner's God, the God of the sick *par excellence*, and the predicate 'saviour', 'redeemer' as it were remains *over* as the predicate of divinity as such: *of what* does such a transformation speak? such a *reduction* of the divine? – To be sure: 'the kingdom of God' has thereby grown larger. Formerly he had only his people, his 'chosen' people. In the meantime, just like his people itself, he has gone abroad, gone wandering about; since then he has sat still nowhere: until at last he is at home everywhere, the great cosmopolitan – until he has got 'the great majority' and half the earth on his side. But the God of the 'great majority', the democrat among gods, has nonetheless not become a proud pagan God: he has remained a Jew, he has remained the God of the nook, the God of all the dark corners and places, of all unhealthy quarters throughout the world! ... His world-empire is as before an underworld-empire, a hospital, a *souterrain*-empire, a ghetto-empire. ... And he himself so pale, so weak, so *décadent*. ... Even the palest of the pale have still been able to master him, *messieurs* the metaphysicians, the conceptual albinos. These have spun their web around him so long that, hypnotized by their movements, he himself became a spider, a metaphysician. Thenceforward he span the world again out of himself – *sub specie Spinozae* – thenceforward he transformed himself into something ever paler and less substantial, became an 'ideal', became 'pure spirit', became '*absolutum*', became 'thing in itself'. ... *Decay of a God*: God became 'thing in itself' ...

18

The Christian conception of God – God as God of the sick, God as spider, God as spirit – is one of the most corrupt conceptions of God arrived at on earth: perhaps it even represents the low-water mark in the descending development of the God type. God degenerated to the *contradiction of life*, instead of being its transfiguration and eternal *Yes*! In God a declaration of hostility towards life, nature, the will to life! God the formula for every calumny of 'this world', for every lie about 'the next world'! In God nothingness deified, the will to nothingness sanctified! ...

19

That the strong races of northern Europe have not repudiated the Christian God certainly reflects no credit on their talent for religion – not to speak of their taste. They ought to have felt *compelled* to have done with such a sickly and decrepit product of *décadence*. But there lies a curse on them for not having had done with it: they have taken up sickness, old age, contradiction into all their instincts – since then they have failed to *create* a God! Almost two millennia and not a single new God! But still, and as if existing by right, like an ultimate and maximum of the God-creating force, of the *creator spiritus* in man, this pitiable God of Christian monotono-theism! This hybrid of the void, conceptualism and contradiction, this picture of decay, in which all *décadence* instincts, all cowardliness and weariness of soul have their sanction! –

20

With my condemnation of Christianity, I should not like to have wronged a kindred religion which even preponderates in the number of its believers: *Buddhism*. They belong together as nihilistic religions – they are *décadence* religions – but they are distinguished from one another in the most remarkable way. The critic of Christianity is profoundly grateful to Indian scholars that one is now able to *compare* these two religions. – Buddhism is a hundred times more realistic than Christianity – it has the heritage of a cool and objective posing of problems in its composition, it arrives *after* a philosophical movement lasting hundreds of years; the concept 'God' is already abolished by the time it arrives. Buddhism is the only really *positivistic* religion history has to show us, even in its epistemology (a strict phenomenalism –), it no longer speaks of 'the struggle against *sin*' but, quite in accordance with actuality, 'the struggle against *suffering*'. It already has – and this distinguishes it profoundly from Christianity – the self-deception of moral concepts behind it – it stands, in my language, *beyond* good and evil. – The *two* physiological facts upon which it rests and on which it fixes its eyes are: *firstly* an excessive excitability of sensibility which expresses itself as a refined capacity for pain, *then* an over-intellectuality, a too great preoccupation with concepts and logical procedures under which the personal instinct has sustained harm to the advantage of the 'impersonal' (– both of them conditions which at any rate some of my readers, the objective ones, will

know from experience, as I do). On the basis of these physiological conditions a state of *depression* has arisen: against this
depression Buddha takes hygienic measures. He opposes it
with life in the open air, the wandering life; with moderation
and fastidiousness as regards food; with caution towards all
alcoholic spirits; likewise with caution towards all emotions
which produce gall, which heat the blood; *no* anxiety, either
for oneself or for others. He demands ideas which produce
repose or cheerfulness – he devises means for disaccustoming
oneself to others. He understands benevolence, being kind,
as health-promoting. *Prayer* is excluded, as is *asceticism*; no
categorical imperative, no *compulsion* at all, not even within the
monastic community (– one can leave it –). All these would
have the effect of increasing that excessive excitability. For
this reason too he demands no struggle against those who
think differently; his teaching resists nothing *more* than it
resists the feeling of revengefulness, of antipathy, of *ressentiment* (– 'enmity is not ended by enmity': the moving refrain of
the whole of Buddhism . . .). And quite rightly: it is precisely
these emotions which would be thoroughly *unhealthy* with regard to the main dietetic objective. The spiritual weariness he
discovered and which expressed itself as an excessive 'objectivity' (that is to say weakening of individual interest, loss of
centre of gravity, of 'egoism'), he combated by directing even
the spiritual interests back to the individual *person*. In the
teaching of Buddha egoism becomes a duty: the 'one thing
needful', the 'how can *you* get rid of suffering' regulates and
circumscribes the entire spiritual diet (– one may perhaps call
to mind that Athenian who likewise made war on pure
'scientificality', Socrates, who elevated personal egoism to
morality even in the domain of problems).

21

The precondition for Buddhism is a very mild climate, very
gentle and liberal customs, *no* militarism; and that it is the
higher and even learned classes in which the movement has its
home. The supreme goal is cheerfulness, stillness, absence of

desire, and this goal is *achieved*. Buddhism is not a religion in which one merely aspires after perfection: perfection is the normal case. –

In Christianity the instincts of the subjugated and oppressed come into the foreground: it is the lowest classes which seek their salvation in it. Here the casuistic *business* of sin, self-criticism, conscience-inquisition is practised as a specific against boredom; here an emotional attitude towards a *power*, called 'God', is kept constantly alive (through prayer); here the highest things are considered unachievable, gifts, 'grace'. Here public openness is also lacking; the hole-and-corner, the dark chamber is Christian. Here the body is despised, hygiene repudiated as sensuality; the Church even resists cleanliness (– the first measure taken by the Christians after the expulsion of the Moors was the closure of the public baths, of which Cordova alone possessed 270). A certain sense of cruelty towards oneself and others is Christian; hatred of those who think differently; the will to persecute. Gloomy and exciting ideas stand in the foreground; the states most highly desired and designated by the highest names are epileptoid states; diet is selected so as to encourage morbid phenomena and to over-excite the nerves. Mortal hostility against the masters of the earth, against the 'noble' – and at the same time a covert secret competition (– one allows them the 'body', one wants *only* the 'soul'): that is also Christian. Hatred of *mind*, of pride, courage, freedom, *libertinage* of mind is Christian; hatred of the *senses*, of the joy of the senses, of joy in general is Christian . . .

22

When it left its original home, the lowest orders, the *underworld* of the ancient world, when it went in search of power among barbarian peoples, Christianity had no longer to pre-suppose *weary* human beings but inwardly savage and self-lacerating ones – strong but ill-constituted human beings. Here discontentedness with oneself, suffering from oneself is *not*, as it is with the Buddhists, an immoderate excitability and capacity for pain, but on the contrary an overwhelming desire to do harm, to discharge an inner tension in hostile actions and ideas. To dominate barbarians Christianity had need of *barbarous* concepts and values: sacrifice of the first-born, blood-drinking at communion, contempt for intellect and culture; torture in all its forms, physical and non-physical; great pomp brought to public worship. Buddhism is a religion for *late* human beings, for races grown kindly, gentle, over-intellectual who feel pain too easily (– Europe is not nearly ripe for it –): it leads them back to peace and cheerfulness, to an ordered diet in intellectual things, to a certain physical hardening. Christianity desires to dominate *beasts of prey*; its means for doing so is to make them *sick* – weakening is the Christian recipe for taming, for 'civilization'. Buddhism is a religion for the end and fatigue of a civilization, Christianity does not even find civilization in existence – it establishes civilization if need be.

23

Buddhism, to say it again, is a hundred times colder, more veracious, more objective. It no longer needs to make its suffering and capacity for pain *decent* to itself by interpreting it as sin – it merely says what it feels: 'I suffer'. To the barbarian, on the contrary, suffering in itself is not decent: he first requires it to be interpreted before he will admit to himself *that* he suffers (his instinct directs him rather to deny he is suffering, to a silent endurance). Here the word 'Devil' was a blessing: one had an overwhelming and fearful enemy – one did not need to be ashamed of suffering at the hands of such an enemy. –

Christianity has a number of subtleties in its foundations which belong to the Orient. Above all, it knows that it is in itself a matter of absolute indifference whether a thing be true, but a matter of the highest importance *to what extent* it is believed to be true. Truth and the *belief* that something is true: two completely diverse worlds of interest, almost *antithetical* worlds – one gets to them by fundamentally different roads. To be knowledgeable in this – in the Orient that is almost enough to *constitute* a sage: thus the Brahmins* understood it, thus Plato understands it, thus does every student of esoteric wisdom understand it. If, for example, there is *happiness* to be found in believing oneself redeemed from sin, it is *not* necessary for a man first to be sinful, but for him to *feel* himself sinful. If, however, it is *belief* as such which is necessary above all else, then one has to bring reason, knowledge, inquiry into disrepute: the road to truth becomes the *forbidden* road. – Intense *hope* is a much stronger stimulant to life than any single instance of happiness which actually occurs. Sufferers have to be sustained by a hope which cannot be refuted by any actuality – which is not *done away with* by any fulfilment: a hope in the Beyond. (It was precisely on account of this capacity for keeping the unhappy in suspense that the Greeks considered hope the evil of evils, the actual *malignant* evil: it remained behind in the box of evil.) – So that *love* shall be possible, God has to be a person; so that the lowest instincts shall have a voice, God has to be young. To satisfy the ardour of the women a handsome saint is moved into the foreground, to satisfy that of the men a Mary. This on the presupposition that Christianity desires to become master on a soil where the worship of Adonis or Aphrodite has already determined the *concept* of what religious worship is. The requirement of *chastity* increases the vehemence and inward intensity of the religious instinct – it renders the cult warmer, more enthusiastic, more soulful. – Love is the state in which man sees things most of all as they are *not*. The illusion-creating force is there at its height, likewise the sweetening and *transforming* force. One endures more when in love than one otherwise would, one tolerates everything. The point was to devise a religion in which love is possible: with that one is beyond the worst that life can offer – one no longer even sees it. – So much for the three Christian virtues faith, hope and charity:† I call them the three Christian *shrewdnesses*. – Buddhism is too late, too positivistic still to be shrewd in this fashion. –

* The highest or priestly caste in the Hindu system.
† 'Charity' is in the Lutheran Bible rendered by the word 'love' ('*Liebe*').

24

I only touch on the problem of the *origin* of Christianity here. The *first* proposition towards its solution is: Christianity can be understood only by referring to the soil out of which it grew – it is *not* a counter-movement against the Jewish instinct, it is actually its logical consequence, one further conclusion of its fear-inspiring logic. In the Redeemer's formula: 'Salvation is of the Jews'. – The *second* proposition is: the psychological type of the Galilean is still recognizable – but only in a completely degenerate form (which is at once a mutilation and an overloading with foreign traits) could it serve the end to which it was put, that of being the type of a *redeemer* of mankind. –

The Jews are the most remarkable nation of world history because, faced with the question of being or not being, they preferred, with a perfectly uncanny conviction, being *at any price*: the price they had to pay was the radical *falsification* of all nature, all naturalness, all reality, the entire inner world as well as the outer. They defined themselves *counter* to all those conditions under which a nation was previously able to live, was *permitted* to live; they made of themselves an antithesis to *natural* conditions – they inverted religion, religious worship, morality, history, psychology one after the other in an irreparable way into the *contradiction of their natural values*. We encounter the same phenomenon again and in unutterably vaster proportions, although only as a copy – the Christian Church, in contrast to the 'nation of saints', renounces all claim to originality. For precisely this reason the Jews are the most *fateful* nation in world history: their after-effect has falsified mankind to such an extent that today the Christian is able to feel anti-Jewish without realizing he is the *ultimate consequence of the Jews*.*

* Christian anti-Semitism was something Nietzsche experienced in his closest relations and associates, and his assertion that Christianity is a product of Judaism and the 'Jewish instinct' cannot therefore be interpreted anti-Semitically: its purpose is to pull the ground from under the Christian tradition of anti-Semitism by insisting on the continuity of the Jewish religion and the Christian. It will be clear from the text that Nietzsche was not a racialist and did not consider the evolution of Judaism a consequence of the Jews' racial make-up.

In my *Genealogy of Morals* I introduced for the first time the psychology of the antithetical concepts of a *noble* morality and a *ressentiment* morality, the latter deriving from a *denial* of the former: but this latter corresponds totally to Judeo-Christian morality. To be able to reject all that represents the *ascending* movement of life, well-constitutedness, power, beauty, self-affirmation on earth, the instinct of *ressentiment* here become genius had to invent *another* world from which that *life-affirmation* would appear evil, reprehensible as such. Considered psychologically, the Jewish nation is a nation of the toughest vital energy which, placed in impossible circumstances, voluntarily, from the profoundest shrewdness in self-preservation, took the side of all *décadence* instincts – *not* as being dominated by them but because it divined in them a power by means of which one can prevail *against* 'the world'. The Jews are the counterparts of *décadents*: they have been compelled to *act* as *décadents* to the point of illusion, they have known, with a *non plus ultra* of histrionic genius, how to place themselves at the head of all *décadence* movements (– as the Christianity of *Paul* –) so as to make of them something stronger than any party *affirmative* of life. For the kind of man who desires to attain power through Judaism and Christianity, the *priestly* kind, *décadence* is only a *means*: this kind of man has a life-interest in making mankind *sick* and in inverting the concepts 'good' and 'evil', 'true' and 'false' in a mortally dangerous and world-calumniating sense. –

25

The history of Israel is invaluable as a typical history of the *denaturalizing* of natural values: I shall indicate five stages in the process. Originally, above all in the period of the Kingdom, Israel too stood in a *correct*, that is to say natural relationship to all things. Their Yaweh was the expression of their consciousness of power, of their delight in themselves, their hopes of themselves: in him they anticipated victory and salvation, with him they trusted that nature would provide what the people needed – above all rain. Yaweh is the God of Israel and *consequently* the God of justice: the logic of every nation that is in power and has a good conscience about it. These two aspects of a nation's self-affirmation find expression in festival worship: it is grateful for the great destiny which has raised it on high, it is grateful towards the year's seasons and all its good fortune with livestock and husbandry. – This state of things long remained the ideal, even after it had been tragically done away with: anarchy within, the Assyrian from without. But the people retained as its supreme desideratum that vision of a king who is a good soldier and an upright judge: as did above all the typical prophet (that is to say critic and satirist of the hour) Isaiah. – But every hope remained unfulfilled. The old God *could* no longer do what he formerly could. One should have let him go. What happened? One altered the conception of him: at this price one retained him. Yaweh the God of 'justice' – *no longer* at one with Israel, an expression of national self-confidence: now only a God bound by conditions. The new conception of him becomes an instrument in the hands of priestly agitators who henceforth interpret all good fortune as a reward, all misfortune as punishment for disobedience of God, for 'sin': that most mendacious mode of interpretation of a supposed 'moral world-order' through which the natural concept 'cause' and 'effect' is once and for all stood on its head. When one has banished natural causality from the world by means of reward and punishment, one then requires an *anti-natural* causality: all the remaining unnaturalness follows forthwith. A God who *demands* – in place of a God who helps, who devises means, who is fundamentally a word for every happy inspiration of courage and self-reliance. . . . *Morality* no longer the expression of the conditions under which a nation lives and grows, no longer a nation's deepest instinct of life, but become abstract, become the antithesis of life – morality as a fundamental degradation of the imagination, as an 'evil eye' for all things. *What* is Jewish, *what* is Christian morality? Chance robbed of its innocence; misfortune dirtied by the concept 'sin'; well-being as a danger, as 'temptation'; physiological indisposition poisoned by the worm of conscience . . .

The concept of God falsified; the concept of morality falsified – the Jewish priesthood did not stop there. The entire *history* of Israel was useless: away with it! – These priests perpetrated that miracle of falsification the documentation of which lies before us in a good part of the Bible: with unparalleled disdain of every tradition, every historical reality, they translated their own national past *into religious terms*, that is to say they made of it a stupid salvation-mechanism of guilt towards Yaweh and punishment, piety towards Yaweh and reward. We would feel this most shameful act of historical falsification much more painfully if millennia of *ecclesiastical* interpretation of history had not made us almost oblivious to the demands of integrity *in historicis*. And the philosophers have seconded the Church: the *lie* of a 'moral world-order' permeates the whole evolution even of the most recent philosophy. What does 'moral world-order' mean? That there exists once and for all a will of God as to what man is to do and what he is not to do; that the value of a nation, of an individual is to be measured by how much or how little obedience is accorded the will of God; that the *ruling power* of the will of God, expressed as punishment and reward according to the degree of obedience, is demonstrated in the destiny of a nation, of an individual. – The *reality* displaced by this pitiable lie is: a parasitic kind of human being which prospers only at the expense of every healthy form of life, the *priest*, abuses the name of God: he calls a state of society in which the priest determines the value of things 'the kingdom of God'; he calls the means by which such a state is achieved or perpetuated 'the will of God'; with cold-blooded cynicism he assesses nations, epochs, individuals according to whether they were conducive to the rule of priests or whether they resisted it. Observe them at work: in the hands of the Jewish priests the *great* epoch in the history of Israel became an epoch of decay, the Exile, the long years of misfortune, was transformed into an eternal *punishment* for the great epoch – an epoch in which the priest was as yet nothing. According to their requirements they made the mighty, *very freely* constituted figures of Israel's history into either pathetic cringing bigots or 'godless men', they simplified the psychology of every great event into the idiotic formula 'obedience to *or* disobedience of God'. – A further step: the 'will of God' (that is to say the conditions for preserving the power of the priest) has to be *known* – to this end a 'revelation' is required. In plain words: a great literary forgery becomes necessary, a 'sacred book' is discovered – it is made public with all hieratic pomp, with days of repentance and with lamentation over the long years of 'sinfulness'. The 'will of God' had been established years before: the whole evil lay in the nation's having become estranged from the 'sacred book'. . . . The 'will of God' had been revealed already to Moses. . . . What had happened? The priest had, with precision and pedantry, right down to the imposts large and small which had to be paid to him (– not forgetting the tastiest pieces of meat: for the priest is a beefeater), formulated once and for all *what he intends to have*, 'what the will of God is'. . . . From now on all things of life are so ordered that the priest is *everywhere indispensable*; at all the natural events of life, at birth, marriage, sickness, death, not to speak of 'sacrifice' (meal-times), there appears the holy parasite to *denaturalize* them – in his language to 'sanctify' them. . . . For one must grasp this: every natural custom, every natural institution (state, administration of justice, marriage, tending of the sick and poor), every requirement presented by the instinct for life, in short everything valuable *in itself*, becomes utterly valueless, *inimical* to value through the parasitism of the priest (or the 'moral world-order'): a sanction is subsequently required – a *value-bestowing* power is needed which denies the natural quality in these things and only by doing so is able to *create* a value. . . . The priest disvalues, *dissanctifies* nature: it is only at the price of this that he exists at all. – Disobedience of God, that is to say of the priest, of 'the Law', now acquires the name 'sin'; the means of 'becoming reconciled again with God' are, as is only to be expected, means by which subjection to the priest is only more thoroughly guaranteed: the priest alone 'redeems'. . . . From a psychological point of view, 'sins' are indispensable in any society organized by priests: they are the actual levers of power, the priest *lives* on sins, he needs 'the commission of sins'. . . . Supreme law: 'God forgives him who repents' – in plain language: *who subjects himself to the priest. –*

27

On a soil *falsified* in this way, where all nature, all natural value, all *reality* had the profoundest instincts of the ruling class against it, there arose *Christianity*, a form of mortal hostility to reality as yet unsurpassed. The 'holy people', which had retained only priestly values, priestly words, for all things, and with a consistency capable of inspiring fear had separated itself from everything else powerful on earth, calling it 'unholy', 'world', 'sin' – this people produced for its instinct a formula which was logical to the point of self-negation: as *Christianity* it negated the last remaining form of reality, the 'holy people', the 'chosen people', the *Jewish* reality itself. The case is of the first rank: the little rebellious movement which is baptised with the name of Jesus of Nazareth is the Jewish instinct *once more* – in other words the priestly instinct which can no longer endure the priest as a reality, the invention of an even *more abstract* form of existence, an even *more unreal* vision of the world than one conditioned by an organized Church. Christianity *negates* the Church . . .

I fail to see against what the revolt was directed whose originator Jesus is understood or *misunderstood* to be if it was not a revolt against the Jewish Church – 'Church' taken in precisely the sense in which we take the word today. It was a revolt against 'the good and the just', against 'the saints of Israel', against the social hierarchy – *not* against a corruption of these but against caste, privilege, the order, the social form; it was *disbelief* in 'higher men', a *No* uttered towards everything that was priest and theologian. But the hierarchy which was thus called in question, even if only momentarily, was the pile-work upon which the Jewish nation continued to exist at all in the midst of the 'waters' – the laboriously-achieved *last* possibility of remaining in being, the residuum of its separate political existence: an attack on this was an attack on the profoundest national instinct, on the toughest national will to life which has ever existed on earth. This holy anarchist who roused up the lowly, the outcasts and 'sinners', the *Chandala* within Judaism to oppose the ruling order – in language which, if the Gospels are to be trusted, would even today lead to Siberia – was a political criminal, in so far as political criminals were possible in an *absurdly unpolitical* society. This is what brought him to the Cross: the proof is the inscription on the Cross. He died for *his* guilt – all ground is lacking for the assertion, however often it is made, that he died for the guilt of others. –

28

It is quite another question whether he was conscious of any such antithesis – whether he was not merely *felt* to be this antithesis. And here for the first time I touch on the problem of the *psychology of the redeemer*. – I confess there are few books which present me with so many difficulties as the Gospels do. These difficulties are quite other than those which the learned curiosity of the German mind celebrated one of its most unforgetable triumphs in pointing out. The time is far distant when I too, like every young scholar and with the clever dullness of a refined philologist, savoured the work of the incomparable Strauss. I was then twenty years old: now I am too serious for that. What do I care for the contradictions of 'tradition'? How can legends of saints be called 'tradition' at all! The stories of saints are the most ambiguous literature in existence: to apply to them scientific procedures *when no other records are extant* seems to me wrong in principle – mere learned idling . . .

29

What *I* am concerned with is the psychological type of the redeemer. For it *could* be contained in the Gospels in spite of the Gospels, however much mutilated and overloaded with foreign traits: as that of Francis of Assisi is contained in the legends about him in spite of the legends. *Not* the truth about what he did, what he said, how he really died: but the question *whether* his type is still conceivable at all, whether it has been 'handed down' by tradition. – The attempts I know of to extract even the *history* of a 'soul' from the Gospels seem to me proofs of an execrable psychological frivolity. Monsieur Renan, that buffoon *in psychologicis*, has appropriated for his explication of the type Jesus the two *most inapplicable* concepts possible in this case: the concept of the *genius* and the concept of the *hero*. But if anything is unevangelic it is the concept hero. Precisely the opposite of all contending, of all feeling oneself in struggle has here become instinct: the incapacity for resistance here becomes morality ('resist not evil!': the profoundest saying of the Gospel, its key in a certain sense), blessedness in peace, in gentleness, in the *inability* for enmity. What are the 'glad tidings'? True life, eternal life is found – it is not promised, it is here, it is *within you*: as life lived in love, in love without deduction or exclusion, without distance. Everyone is a child of God – Jesus definitely claims nothing for himself alone – as a child of God everyone is equal to everyone else. . . . To make a *hero* of Jesus! – And what a worse misunderstanding is the word 'genius'! Our whole concept, our cultural concept 'spirit' had no meaning whatever in the world Jesus lived in. To speak with the precision of the physiologist a quite different word would rather be in place here: the word idiot. We recognize a condition of morbid susceptibility of the *sense of touch* which makes it shrink back in horror from every contact, every grasping of a firm object. Translate such a physiological *habitus*** into its ultimate logic – as instinctive hatred of *every* reality, as flight into the 'ungraspable', into the 'inconceivable', as antipathy towards every form, every spacial and temporal concept, towards everything firm, all that is custom, institution, Church, as being at home in a world undisturbed by reality of any kind, a merely 'inner world, a 'real' world, an 'eternal' world. . . . 'The kingdom of God *is within you*' . . .

* condition.

30

Instinctive hatred of reality: consequence of an extreme capacity for suffering and irritation which no longer wants to be 'touched' at all because it feels every contact too deeply.

Instinctive exclusion of all aversion, all enmity, all feeling for limitation and distancing: consequence of an extreme capacity for suffering and irritation which already feels all resisting, all need for resistance, as an unbearable *displeasure* (that is to say as *harmful*, as *deprecated* by the instinct of self-preservation) and knows blessedness (pleasure) only in no longer resisting anyone or anything, neither the evil nor the evil-doer – love as the sole, as the *last* possibility of life . . .

These are the two *physiological realities* upon which, out of which the doctrine of redemption has grown. I call it a sublime further evolution of hedonism on a thoroughly morbid basis. Closest related to it, even if with a considerable addition of Greek vitality and nervous energy, is Epicureanism, the redemption doctrine of the pagan world. Epicurus a *typical décadent*: first recognized as such by me. – The fear of pain, even of the infinitely small in pain – *cannot* end otherwise than in a *religion of love* . . .

31

I have anticipated my answer to the problem. Its presupposition is that the type of the redeemer has been preserved to us only in a very distorted form. That this distortion should have occurred is in itself very probable: there are several reasons why such a type could not remain pure, whole, free of accretions. The milieu in which this strange figure moved must have left its mark upon him, as must even more the history, the *fate* of the first Christian community: from this the type was retrospectively enriched with traits which become comprehensible only with reference to warfare and the aims of propaganda. That strange and sick world to which the Gospels introduce us – a world like that of a Russian novel, in which refuse of society, neurosis and 'childlike' idiocy seem to make a rendezvous – must in any case have *coarsened* the type: the first disciples in particular had to translate a being immersed entirely in symbols and incomprehensibilities into their own crudity in order to understand anything of it at all – for them such a type could not *exist* until it had been reduced to more familiar forms. . . . The prophet, the Messiah, the judge who is to come, the moral preacher, the miracle-worker, John the Baptist – so many opportunities for misunderstanding the type. . . . Finally, let us not underestimate the *proprium** of all extreme, and in particular sectarian veneration: it extinguishes the original often painfully unfamiliar traits and idiosyncrasies in the revered being – *it even fails to see them*. One has to regret that no Dostoyevsky lived in the neighbourhood of this most interesting *décadent*; I mean someone who could feel the thrilling fascination of such a combination of the sublime, the sick and the childish. One final viewpoint: the type, as a *décadence* type, *could* in fact have been of a peculiar multiplicity and contradictoriness: such a possibility cannot be entirely excluded. But everything speaks against it: for if it were so the tradition would have to have been remarkably faithful and objective: and we have reasons for assuming the opposite. In the meantime, there yawns a contradiction between the mountain, lake and field preacher, whose appearance strikes one as that of a Buddha on a soil very little like that of India, and the aggressive fanatic, the mortal enemy of theologian and priest, which Renan has wickedly glorified as '*le grand maitre en ironie*'. I myself have no doubt that this plentiful measure of gall (and even of *esprit*) has only overflowed on to the type of the Master out of the excited condition of Christian propaganda: for one knows very well how resolutely all sectarians adjust their Master into an apologia of themselves. When the first community had need of a censuring theologian to oppose the theologians they *created* their 'God' according to their requirements: just as they unhesitatingly put into his mouth those totally unevangelic concepts which they could not now do without, 'Second Coming', 'Last Judgement', every kind of temporal promise and expectation. –

* characteristic.

I resist, to repeat it, the incorporation of the fanatic into the type of the redeemer: the word *impérieux* alone which Renan employs already *annuls* the type. The 'glad tidings' are precisely that there are no more opposites; the kingdom of Heaven belongs to *children*; the faith which here finds utterance is not a faith which has been won by struggle – it is there, from the beginning, it is as it were a return to childishness in the spiritual domain. The occurrence of retarded puberty undeveloped in the organism as a consequence of degeneration is familiar at any rate to physiologists. – Such a faith is not angry, does not censure, does not defend itself: it does not bring 'the sword' – it has no idea to what extent it could one day cause dissention. It does not prove itself, either by miracles or by rewards and promises, and certainly not 'by the Scriptures': it is every moment its own miracle, its own reward, its own proof, its own 'kingdom of God'. Neither does this faith formulate itself – it *lives*, it resists formulas. Chance, to be sure, determines the environment, the language, the preparatory schooling of a particular configuration of concepts: primitive Christianity employs *only* Judeo-Semitic concepts (– eating and drinking at communion belong here, concepts so sadly abused, like everything Jewish, by the Church). But one must be careful not to see in this anything but a sign-language, a semeiotic, an occasion for metaphors. It is precisely on condition that nothing he says is taken literally that this antirealist can speak at all. Among Indians he would have made use of Sankhyam concepts, among Chinese those of Lao-tse – and would not have felt the difference. – One could, with some freedom of expression, call Jesus a 'free spirit' – he cares nothing for what is fixed: the word *killeth*, everything fixed *killeth*. The concept, the *experience* 'life' in the only form he knows it is opposed to any kind of word, formula, law, faith, dogma. He speaks only of the inmost thing: 'life' or 'truth' or 'light' is his expression for the inmost thing – everything else, the whole of reality, the whole of nature, language itself, possesses for him merely the value of a sign, a metaphor. – On this point one must make absolutely no mistake, however much Christian, that is to say *ecclesiastical* prejudice, may tempt one to do so: such a symbolist *par excellence* stands outside of all religion, all conceptions of divine worship, all history, all natural science, all experience of the world, all acquirements, all politics, all psychology, all books, all art – his 'knowledge' is precisely the *pure folly* of the fact *that* anything of this kind exists. He has not so much as heard of *culture*, he does not need to fight against it – he does not deny it. . . . The same applies to the *state*, to society and the entire civic order, to *work*, to war – he never had reason to deny 'the world', he had no notion of the ecclesiastical concept 'world'. . . . *Denial* is precisely what is totally impossible for him. – Dialectics are likewise lacking, the idea is lacking that a faith, a 'truth' could be proved by reasons (– *his* proofs are inner 'lights', inner feelings of pleasure and self-affirmations, nothing but 'proofs by potency' –). Neither *can* such a doctrine argue: it simply does not understand that other doctrines exist, *can* exist, it simply does not know how to imagine an opinion contrary to its own. . . . Where it encounters one it will, with the most heartfelt sympathy, lament the 'blindness' – for it sees the 'light' – but it will make no objection . . .

33

In the entire psychology of the 'Gospel' the concept guilt and punishment is lacking; likewise the concept reward. 'Sin', every kind of distancing relationship between God and man, is abolished – *precisely this is the 'glad tidings'*. Blessedness is not promised, it is not tied to any conditions: it is the *only* reality – the rest is signs for speaking of it . . .

The *consequence* of such a condition projects itself into a new *practice*, the true evangelic practice. It is not a 'belief' which distinguishes the Christian: the Christian acts, he is distinguished by a *different* mode of acting. Neither by words nor in his heart does he resist the man who does him evil. He makes no distinction between foreigner and native, between Jew and non-Jew ('one's neighbour' is properly one's co-religionist, the Jew). He is not angry with anyone, does not disdain any-one. He neither appears in courts of law nor claims their protection ('not swearing'). Under no circumstances, not even in the case of proved unfaithfulness, does he divorce his wife. – All fundamentally *one* law, all consequences of *one* instinct. –

The life of the redeemer was nothing else than *this* practice – his death too was nothing else. . . . He no longer required any formulas, any rites for communicating with God – not even prayer. He has settled his accounts with the whole Jewish penance-and-reconciliation doctrine; he knows that it is through the *practice* of one's life that one feels 'divine', 'blessed', 'evangelic', at all times a 'child of God'. It is *not* 'penance', *not* 'prayer for forgiveness' which leads to God: *evangelic practice alone* leads to God, it *is* God! – What was *abolished* with the Evangel was the Judaism of the concepts 'sin', 'forgiveness of sin', 'faith', 'redemption by faith' – the whole of Jewish *ecclesiastical* teaching was denied in the 'glad tidings'.

The profound instinct for how one would have to *live* in order to feel oneself 'in Heaven', to feel oneself 'eternal', while in every other condition one by *no* means feels oneself 'in Heaven': this alone is the psychological reality of 'redemption'. – A new way of living, *not* a new belief . . .

34

If I understand anything of this great symbolist it is that he took for realities, for 'truths', only *inner* realities – that he understood the rest, everything pertaining to nature, time, space, history, only as signs, as occasion for metaphor. The concept 'the Son of Man' is not a concrete person belonging to history, anything at all individual or unique, but an 'eternal' fact, a psychological symbol freed from the time concept. The same applies supremely to the *God* of this typical symbolist, to the 'kingdom of God', to the 'kingdom of Heaven', to 'God's children'. Nothing is more un-Christian than the *ecclesiastical crudities* of a God as a *person*, of a 'kingdom of God' which *comes*, of a 'kingdom of Heaven' in the *Beyond*, of a 'Son of God', the *second person* of the Trinity. All this is – forgive the expression – a *fist* in the eye* – oh in what an eye! – of the Gospel: *world-historical cynicism* in the mockery of symbolism. . . . But it is patently obvious what is alluded to in the symbols 'Father' and 'Son' – not patently obvious to everyone, I grant: in the word 'Son' is expressed the *entry* into the collective feeling of the transfiguration of all things (blessedness), in the word 'Father' *this feeling itself*, the feeling of perfection and eternity. – I am ashamed to recall what the Church has made of this symbolism: has it not set an Amphitryon† story at the threshold of Christian 'faith'? And a dogma of 'immaculate conception' into the bargain? . . . *But it has thereby maculated conception* –

The 'kingdom of Heaven' is a condition of the heart – not something that comes 'upon the earth' or 'after death'. The entire concept of natural death is *lacking* in the Gospel: death is not a bridge, not a transition, it is lacking because it belongs to quite another world, a merely apparent world useful only for the purpose of symbolism. The 'hour of death' is *not* a Christian concept – the 'hour', time, physical life and its crises, simply do not exist for the teacher of the 'glad tidings'. . . . The 'kingdom of God' is not something one waits for; it has no yesterday or tomorrow, it does not come 'in a thousand years' – it is an experience within a heart; it is everywhere, it is nowhere . . .

35

This 'bringer of glad tidings' died as he lived, as he *taught* – *not* to 'redeem mankind' but to demonstrate how one ought to live. What he bequeathed to mankind is his *practice*: his bearing before the judges, before the guards, before the accusers and every kind of calumny and mockery – his

---

* 'That is as fitting as a fist in the eye' is a German idiom meaning a complete unlikeness between two things – 'alike as chalk and cheese'.

† Amphitryon's wife Alcmene refused to sleep with him until he had revenged the death of her brothers; while Amphitryon was away engaged on this task his still virgin bride was seduced by Zeus and subsequently gave birth to Heracles.

bearing on the *Cross*. He does not resist, he does not defend his rights, he takes no steps to avert the worst that can happen to him – more, *he provokes it*. . . . And he entreats, he suffers, he loves *with* those, *in* those who are doing evil to him. His words to the *thief* on the cross contain the whole Evangel. 'That was verily a *divine* man, a child of God!' – says the thief. 'If thou feelest this' – answers the redeemer – '*thou art in Paradise*, thou art a child of God.' *Not* to defend oneself, *not* to grow angry, *not* to make responsible. . . . But not to resist even the evil man – to *love* him . . .

36

– Only we, we *emancipated* spirits, possess the prerequisite for understanding something nineteen centuries have misunderstood – that integrity become instinct and passion which makes war on the 'holy lie' even more than on any other lie. . . . One has been unspeakably far from our benevolent and cautious neutrality, from that discipline of the spirit through which alone the divining of such strange, such delicate things is made possible: at all times one has, with shameless self-seeking, desired only *one's own* advantage in these things, one constructed the *Church* out of the antithesis to the Gospel.

If anyone were looking for a sign that an ironical divinity was at work behind the great universal drama he would find no small support in the *tremendous question-mark* called Christianity. That mankind should fall on its knees before the opposite of what was the origin, the meaning, the *right* of the Gospel, that it should have sanctified in the concept 'Church' precisely what the 'bringer of glad tidings' regarded as *beneath* him, *behind* him – one seeks in vain a grander form of *world-historical irony* –

37

– Our age is proud of its historical sense: how was it able to make itself believe in the nonsensical notion that the *crude miracle-worker and redeemer fable* comes at the commencement of Christianity – and that everything spiritual and symbolic is only a subsequent development? On the contrary: the history of Christianity – and that from the very death on the Cross – is the history of progressively cruder misunderstanding of an *original* symbolism. With every extension of Christianity over even broader, even ruder masses in whom the preconditions out of which it was born were more and more lacking, it became increasingly necessary to *vulgarize*, to *barbarize* Christianity – it absorbed the doctrines and rites of every *subterranean* cult of the *Imperium Romanum*, it absorbed the absurdities of every sort of morbid reason. The fate of Christianity lies in the necessity for its faith itself to grow as morbid, low and vulgar as the requirements it was intended to satisfy were morbid, low and vulgar. As the Church, this *morbid barbarism* itself finally assumes power – the Church, that form of mortal hostility to all integrity, to all *loftiness* of soul, to discipline of spirit, to all open-hearted and benevolent humanity. – *Christian* values – *noble* values: it is only we, we *emancipated* spirits, who have restored this greatest of all value-antitheses! –

38

– At this point I shall not suppress a sigh. There are days when I am haunted by a feeling blacker than the blackest melancholy – *contempt of man*. And so as to leave no doubt as to *what* I despise, *whom* I despise: it is the man of today, the man with whom I am fatefully contemporary. The man of today – I suffocate of his impure breath. . . . With regard to the past I am, like all men of knowledge, of a large tolerance, that is to say a *magnanimous* self-control: I traverse the madhouse-world of entire millennia, be it called 'Christianity', 'Christian faith', 'Christian Church', with a gloomy circumspection – I take care not to make mankind responsible for its insanities. But my feelings suddenly alter, burst forth, immediately I enter the modern age, *our* age. Our age *knows*. . . . What was formerly merely morbid has today become indecent – it is indecent to be a Christian today. *And here is where my disgust commences.* – I look around me: there is no longer a word left of what was formerly called 'truth', we no longer endure it when a priest so much as utters the word 'truth'. Even with the most modest claim to integrity one *must* know today that a theologian, a priest, a pope does not merely err in every sentence he speaks, he *lies* – that he is no longer free to lie 'innocently', out of 'ignorance'. The priest knows as well as anyone that there is no longer any 'God', any 'sinner', any 'redeemer' – that 'free will', 'moral world-order' are lies – intellectual seriousness, the profound self-overcoming of the intellect, no longer *permits* anyone *not* to know about these things. . . . *All* the concepts of the Church are recognized for what they are: the most malicious false-coinage there is for the purpose of *dis-valuing* nature and natural values; the priest himself is recognized for what he is: the most dangerous kind of parasite, the actual poison-spider of life. . . . We know, our *conscience* knows today – *what* those sinister inventions of priest and Church are worth, *what end they serve*, with which that state of human self-violation has been brought about which is capable of exciting disgust at the sight of mankind – the concepts 'Beyond', 'Last Judgement', 'immortality of the soul', the 'soul' itself: they are instruments of torture, they are forms of systematic cruelty by virtue of which the priest has become master, stays master. . . . Everyone knows this: *and everyone nonetheless remains unchanged*. Where have the last feelings of decency and self-respect gone when even our statesmen, in other ways a very unprejudiced kind of man and practical anti-Christians through and through, still call themselves Christians today and go to Communion? . . . A young prince at the head of his regiments, splendid as the expression of his people's egoism and presumption – but *without* any shame professing himself a Christian! . . . *Whom* then does Christianity deny? *what* does it call 'world'? Being a soldier, being a judge, being a patriot; defending oneself; preserving one's honour; desiring to seek one's advantage; being *proud*. . . . The practice of every hour, every instinct, every valuation which leads to *action* is today anti-Christian: what a *monster of falsity* modern man must be that he is nonetheless *not ashamed* to be called a Christian!

– To resume, I shall now relate the *real* history of Christianity.
– The word 'Christianity' is already a misunderstanding – in
reality there has been only one Christian, and he died on the
Cross. The 'Evangel' *died* on the Cross. What was called
'Evangel' from this moment onwards was already the oppo-
site of what *he* had lived: '*bad* tidings', a *dysangel*. It is false to
the point of absurdity to see in a 'belief', perchance the belief
in redemption through Christ, the distinguishing characteristic of the Christian: only Christian *practice*, a life such as he
who died on the Cross *lived*, is Christian. . . . Even today *such* a
life is possible, for *certain* men even necessary: genuine,
primitive Christianity will be possible at all times. . . . *Not* a
belief but a doing, above all a *not*-doing of many things, a
different *being*. . . . States of consciousness, beliefs of any kind,
holding something to be true for example – every psychologist
knows this – are a matter of complete indifference and of the
fifth rank compared with the value of the instincts: to speak
more strictly, the whole concept of spiritual causality is false.
To reduce being a Christian, Christianness, to a holding
something to be true, to a mere phenomenality of consciousness, means to negate Christianness. *In fact there have been no
Christians at all*. The 'Christian', that which has been called
Christian for two millennia, is merely a psychological self-
misunderstanding. Regarded more closely, that which has
ruled in him, *in spite of* all his 'faith', has been *merely* the instincts – and what instincts! 'Faith' has been at all times, with
Luther for instance, only a cloak, a pretext, a *screen*, behind
which the instincts played their game – a shrewd *blindness* to
the dominance of *certain* instincts. . . . 'Faith' – I have already
called it the true Christian *shrewdness* – one has always *spoken* of
faith, one has always *acted* from instinct. . . . The Christian's
world of ideas contains nothing which so much as touches
upon actuality: on the other hand, we have recognized in
instinctive hatred *for* actuality the driving element, the only
driving element in the roots of Christianity. What follows
therefrom? That here, *in psychologicis* also, error is radical, that

is to say determinant of the essence, that is to say *substance*. *One* concept removed, a single reality substituted in its place – and the whole of Christianity crumbles to nothing! – From a lofty standpoint, this strangest of all facts, a religion not only determined by errors but inventive and even possessing genius *only* in harmful, *only* in life-poisoning and heart-poisoning errors, remains a *spectacle for the gods* – for those divinities which are at the same time philosophers and which I encountered, for example, during those celebrated dialogues on Naxos. In the hour when their *disgust* leaves them (– *and* leaves us!) they become grateful for the spectacle of the Christian: perhaps it is only for the sake of *this* curious case that the pathetic little star called Earth deserves a divine glance and divine participation. . . . For let us not undervalue the Christian: the Christian, false *to the point of innocence*, far surpasses the ape – with respect to Christians a well-known theory of descent becomes a mere compliment . . .

40

– The fate of the Evangel was determined by the death – it hung on the Cross. . . . It was only the death, this unexpected shameful death, only the Cross, which was in general reserved for the *canaille* alone – it was only this terrible paradox which brought the disciples face to face with the real enigma: '*Who was that? What was that?*' – The feeling of being shaken and disappointed to their depths, the suspicion that such a death might be the *refutation* of their cause, the frightful question-mark 'why has this happened?' – this condition is only too understandable. Here everything *had* to be necessary, meaningful, reasonable, reasonable in the highest degree; a disciple's love knows nothing of chance. Only now did the chasm open up: '*Who* killed him? *who* was his natural enemy?' – this question came like a flash of lightning. Answer: *ruling* Judaism, its upper class. From this moment one felt oneself in mutiny *against* the social order, one subsequently understood Jesus as having been *in mutiny against the social order*. Up till then this warlike trait, this negative trait in word and deed,

was *lacking* in his image; more, he was the contradiction of it.
Clearly the little community had *failed* to understand precisely
the main thing, the exemplary element in his manner of
dying, the freedom from, the superiority *over* every feeling of
ressentiment: – a sign of how little they understood of him at
all! Jesus himself could have desired nothing by his death but
publicly to offer the sternest test, the *proof* of his teaching. . . .
But his disciples were far from *forgiving* his death – which would
have been evangelic in the highest sense; not to speak of
offering themselves up to a similar death in sweet and gentle
peace of heart. . . . Precisely the most unevangelic of feelings,
revengefulness, again came uppermost. The affair could not
possibly be at an end with this death: one required 'retribution',
'judgement' (– and yet what can be more unevangelic than
'retribution', 'punishment', 'sitting in judgement'!). The
popular expectation of a Messiah came once more into the
foreground; an historic moment appeared in view: the 'kingdom of God' is coming to sit in judgement on its enemies. . . .
But with this everything is misunderstood: the 'kingdom of
God' as a last act, as a promise! For the Evangel had been
precisely the existence, the fulfilment, the *actuality* of this
'kingdom'. Such a death *was* precisely this 'kingdom of God'.
Only now was all that contempt for and bitterness against
Pharisee and theologian worked into the type of the Master –
one thereby *made* of him a Pharisee and theologian! On the
other hand, the enraged reverence of these utterly unhinged
souls could no longer endure that evangelic equal right of
everyone to be a child of God which Jesus had taught, and
their revenge consisted in *exalting* Jesus in an extravagant
fashion, in severing him from themselves: just as the Jews, in
revenge on their enemies, had previously separated their God
from themselves and raised him on high. The *one* God and the
one Son of God: both products of *ressentiment* . . .

41

– And now an absurd problem came up: 'How *could* God have
permitted that?' For this question the deranged reason of the

153

little community found a downright terrifyingly absurd answer: God gave his Son for the forgiveness of sins, as a *sacrifice*. All at once it was all over with the Gospel! The *guilt sacrifice*, and that in its most repulsive, barbaric form, the sacrifice of the *innocent man* for the sins of the guilty! What atrocious paganism! – For Jesus had done away with the concept 'guilt' itself – he had denied any chasm between God and man, he *lived* this unity of God and man as *his* 'glad tidings'. . . . And *not* as a special prerogative! – From now on there is introduced into the type of the redeemer step by step: the doctrine of a Judgement and a Second Coming, the doctrine of his death as a sacrificial death, the doctrine of the Resurrection with which the entire concept 'blessedness', the whole and sole reality of the Evangel, is juggled away – for the benefit of a state *after* death! . . . Paul, with that rabbinical insolence which characterizes him in every respect, rationalized this interpretation, this *indecency* of an interpretation, thus: '*If* Christ is not resurrected from the dead our faith is vain'. – All at once the Evangel became the most contemptible of all unfulfillable promises, the *impudent* doctrine of personal immortality. . . . Paul himself even taught it as a *reward*! . . .

42

One sees *what* came to an end with the death on the Cross: a new, an absolutely primary beginning to a Buddhistic peace movement, to an actual and *not* merely promised *happiness on earth*. For this remains – I have already emphasized it – the basic distinction between the two *décadence* religions: Buddhism makes no promises but keeps them, Christianity makes a thousand promises but *keeps none*. – On the heels of the 'glad tidings' came the *worst of all*: those of Paul. In Paul was embodied the antithetical type to the 'bringer of glad tidings', the genius of hatred, of the vision of hatred, of the inexorable logic of hatred. *What* did this dysangelist not sacrifice to his hatred! The redeemer above all: he nailed him to *his* Cross. The life, the example, the teaching, the death, the meaning and the right of the entire Gospel – nothing was left once this hate-obsessed false-coiner had grasped what alone he could make use of. *Not* the reality, *not* the historical truth! ... And once more the priestly instinct of the Jew perpetrated the same great crime against history – it simply erased the yesterday and the day before yesterday of Christianity, *it devised for itself a history of primitive Christianity*. More: it falsified the history of Israel over again so as to make this history seem the pre-history of *its* act: all the prophets had spoken of *its* 'redeemer'. ... The Church subsequently falsified even the history of mankind into the pre-history of Christianity. ... The type of the redeemer, the doctrine, the practice, the death, the meaning of the death, even the sequel to the death – nothing was left untouched, nothing was left bearing even the remotest resemblance to reality. Paul simply shifted the centre of gravity of that entire existence *beyond* this existence – in the *lie* of the 'resurrected' Jesus. In fact he could make no use at all of the redeemer's life – he needed the death on the Cross *and* something in addition. ... To regard as honest a Paul whose home was the principal centre of Stoic enlightenment when he makes of a hallucination the *proof* that the redeemer is *still* living, or even to believe his story *that* he had this hallucination, would be a real *niaiserie* on the part of a psychologist: Paul willed the end, *consequently* he willed the means. ... What he himself did not believe was believed by the idiots among whom he cast *his* teaching. – *His* requirement was *power*; with Paul the priest again sought power – he could employ only those concepts, teachings, symbols with which one tyrannizes over masses, forms herds. *What* was the only thing Mohammed later borrowed from Christianity? The invention of Paul, his means for establishing a priestly tyranny, for forming herds: the belief in immortality – *that is to say the doctrine of 'judgement'* ...

43

If one shifts the centre of gravity of life *out* of life into the 'Beyond' – into *nothingness* – one has deprived life as such of its centre of gravity. The great lie of personal immortality destroys all rationality, all naturalness of instinct – all that is salutary, all that is life-furthering, all that holds a guarantee of the future in the instincts henceforth excites mistrust. *So to live that there is no longer any meaning in living: that* now becomes the 'meaning' of life. . . . What is the point of public spirit, what is the point of gratitude for one's descent and one's forefathers, what is the point of co-operation, trust, of furthering and keeping in view the general welfare? . . . So many 'temptations', so many diversions from the 'right road' – '*one thing* is needful'. . . . That, as an 'immortal soul', everybody is equal to everybody else, that in the totality of beings the 'salvation' of *every* single one is permitted to claim to be of everlasting moment, that little bigots and three-quarters madmen are permitted to imagine that for their sakes the laws of nature are continually being *broken* – such a raising of every sort of egoism to infinity, to *impudence*, cannot be branded with sufficient contempt. And yet it is to *this* pitiable flattery of personal vanity that Christianity owes its *victory* – it is with this that it has persuaded over to its side everything ill-constituted, rebellious-minded, under-privileged, all the dross and refuse of mankind. 'Salvation of the soul' – in plain words: 'The world revolves around *me*'. . . . The poison of the doctrine '*equal* rights for all' – this has been more thoroughly sowed by Christianity than by anything else; from the most secret recesses of base instincts, Christianity has waged a war to the death against every feeling of reverence and distance between man and man, against, that is, the *precondition* of every elevation, every increase in culture – it has forged out of the *ressentiment* of the masses its *chief weapon* against *us*, against everything noble, joyful, high-spirited on earth, against our happiness on earth. . . . 'Immortality' granted to every Peter and Paul has been the greatest and most malicious outrage on *noble* mankind ever committed. – *And* let us not underestimate the fatality that has crept out of Christianity even into politics! No one any longer possesses today the courage to claim special privileges or the right to rule, the courage to feel a sense of reverence towards himself and towards his equals – the courage for a *pathos of distance*. . . . Our politics is *morbid* from this lack of courage! – The aristocratic outlook has been undermined most deeply by the lie of equality of souls; and if the belief in the 'prerogative of the majority' makes revolutions and *will continue to make them* – it is Christianity, let there be no doubt about it, *Christian* value judgement which translates every revolution into mere blood and crime! Christianity is a revolt of everything that crawls along the ground directed against that which is *elevated*: the Gospel of the 'lowly' *makes low* . . .

44

– The Gospels are invaluable as evidence of the already irresistible corruption *within* the first community. What Paul later carried to its conclusion with the cynical logic of a rabbi was nonetheless merely the process of decay which commenced with the death of the redeemer. – One cannot read these Gospels too warily; there are difficulties behind every word. I hope I shall be pardoned for confessing that they are for that very reason a pleasure of the first rank to a psychologist – as the *opposite* of all kinds of naïve depravity, as refinement *par excellence*, as artistry in psychological depravity. The Gospels are in a class by themselves. The Bible in general admits of no comparison. One is among Jews: *first* consideration if one is not to lose the thread completely. This self-pretence of 'holiness', which here becomes downright genius and which has not since been even approximately equalled among books and men, this false-coinage of word and attitude as an *art*, is not the chance product of some individual talent, some exceptional nature. *Race* is required for it. In Christianity, as the art of holy lying, the whole of Judaism, a schooling and technique pursued with the utmost seriousness for hundreds of years, attains its ultimate perfection. The Christian, that *ultima ratio* of the lie, is the Jew once more – even *thrice* more. . . . The will to employ as a matter of principle only concepts, symbols, attitudes manifested in the practice of the priest, the instinctive rejection of every *other* practice, every *other* kind of perspective in the realm of values and practical application – that is not tradition, it is *inheritance*: only as inheritance does it have the effect of a natural quality.

The whole of mankind, even the finest heads of the finest epochs (with one exception, who is perhaps merely a monster –) have allowed themselves to be deceived. The Gospel has been read as the *Book of Innocence*. . . . no small pointer to the degree of histrionic mastery displayed in it. – If we got to *see* them, to be sure, even if only in passing, all these singular bigots and artificial saints, it would be the end of them – and it is precisely because *I* never read a word without seeing an attitude that *I make an end of them*. . . . They have a way of raising their eyes to Heaven which I cannot endure. – Fortunately books are for most people merely *literature*. – One must not let oneself be misled: they say ' Judge not!' but they send to Hell everything that stands in their way. By allowing God to judge they themselves judge; by glorifying God they glorify themselves; by *demanding* precisely those virtues of which they themselves are capable – more, which they are in need of to stay on top at all – they present a great appearance of contending for virtue, of struggling for the triumph of virtue. 'We live, we die, we sacrifice ourselves *for the good*' (– 'truth', 'the light', the 'kingdom of God'): in reality they do what they cannot help doing. By making their way in a sneaking fashion, sitting in corners, living out shadowy lives in the shadows, they make a *duty* of it: their life of humility appears to be a duty, as humility it is one more proof of piety. . . . Ah this humble, chaste, compassionate mode of mendaciousness! 'For us virtue itself shall bear witness'. . . . Read the Gospels as books of seduction by means of *morality*: these petty people have placed a distraint on morality– they know what use it can be put to! Mankind can best be *led by the nose* with morality! – The reality is that here the most conscious *arrogance of the elect* is posing as modesty: one has placed *oneself*, the 'community', the 'good and just', once and for all on one side, on the side of 'truth' – and the rest, 'the world', on the other. . . . *That* has been the most fateful kind of megalomania that has ever existed on earth: little abortions of bigots and liars began to lay claim to the concepts 'God', 'truth', 'light', 'spirit', 'love', 'wisdom', 'life' as if these were synonyms of themselves so as to divide themselves off from the 'world'; little superlatives of Jews, ripe for every kind of madhouse, twisted values in general to suit *themselves*, as if only the 'Christian' were the meaning, the salt, the measure and also the *ultimate tribunal* of all the rest. . . . The whole fatality was possible only because there was already in the world a related, racially-related megalomania, the *Jewish*: once the chasm between Jews and Jewish Christians opened up, the latter were left with no alternative but to employ *against* the Jews the very self-preservative procedures counselled by the Jewish instinct, while the Jews had previously employed them only against everything *non*-Jewish. The Christian is only a Jew of a '*freer*' confession. –

45

– I give a few examples of what these petty people have taken into their heads, what they *have put into the mouth* of their Master: confessions of 'beautiful souls' one and all. –

'And whosoever shall not receive you, nor hear you, when ye depart thence, shake off the dust under your feet for a testimony against them. Verily I say unto you, It shall be more tolerable for Sodom and Gomorrha in the day of judgement, than for that city.' (Mark vi, 11) – How evangelic! . . .

'And whosoever shall offend one of these little ones that believe in me, it is better for him that a millstone were hanged about his neck, and he were cast into the sea.' (Mark ix, 42) – How evangelic! . . .

'And if thine eye offend thee, pluck it out; it is better for thee to enter into the kingdom of God with one eye, than having two eyes to be cast into hell fire: Where their worm dieth not, and the fire is not quenched.' (Mark ix, 47–8) – It is not precisely the eye that is meant . . .

'Verily I say unto you, That there be some of them that stand here, which shall not taste of death, till they have seen the kingdom of God come with power.' (Mark ix, 1) – Well *lied*, lion . . .

'Whosoever will come after me, let him deny himself, and take up his cross, and follow me. *For* . . .' (*Observation of a psychologist*: Christian morality is refuted by its *fors*: its 'reasons' refute – thus is it Christian.) Mark viii, 34–5.

'Judge not, *that* ye be not judged. For with what judgement ye judge, *ye* shall be judged.' (Matthew vii, 1–2) – What a conception of justice, of a 'just' judge! ...

'For if ye love them which love you, *what reward have ye*? do not even the publicans do the same? And if ye salute your brethren only what do ye *more than others*? do not even the publicans so?' (Matthew v, 46–7) – Principle of 'Christian love': it wants to be well *paid* ...

'But if ye forgive not men their trespasses, neither will your Father forgive your trespasses.' (Matthew vi, 15) – Very compromising for the said 'Father' ...

'But seek ye first the kingdom of God, and his righteousness; and all these things shall be added unto you.' (Matthew vi, 33) – All these things: namely food, clothing, all the essentials of life. An *error*, to put it mildly. ... A little earlier God appears as a tailor, at least under certain circumstances* ...

'Rejoice ye in that day, and leap for joy: *for* behold, your reward is great in heaven: for in the like manner did their fathers unto the prophets.' (Luke vi, 23) – Impudent rabble! It already compares itself with the prophets. ...

'Know ye not that ye are the temple of God, and that the Spirit of God dwelleth in you? If any man defile the temple of God, *him shall God destroy*; for the temple of God is holy, *which temple ye are*.' (1 Corinthians iii, 16–17) – Such things as this cannot be sufficiently despised ...

'Do ye not know that the saints shall judge the world? and if the world shall be judged by *you*, are ye unworthy to judge the smallest matters?' (1 Corinthians vi, 2) – Unfortunately not merely the ravings of a lunatic. ... This *frightful impostor* goes on to say: 'Know ye not that we shall judge angels? how much more things that pertain to this life?' ...

'Hath not God made foolish the wisdom of this world? For after that in the wisdom of God the world by wisdom knew not God, it pleased God by the foolishness of preaching to save them that believe ... ; not many wise men after the

* Matthew vi, 28–30.

flesh, not many mighty, not many noble, are called: *But God hath chosen* the foolish things of the world to confound the wise; and God hath chosen the weak things of the world to confound the things which are mighty; And base things of the world, and things which are despised, hath God chosen, yea, and things which are not, to bring to naught things that are: That no flesh should glory in his presence.' (1 Corinthians i, 20 ff.) – To *understand* this passage, a document of the very first rank for the psychology of every Chandala morality, one should read the first essay of my *Genealogy of Morals*, where the antithesis between a *noble* morality and a Chandala morality born of *ressentiment* and impotent revengefulness is first brought to light. Paul was the greatest of all apostles of revenge . . .

46

– *What follows from all this?* That one does well to put gloves on when reading the New Testament. The proximity of so much uncleanliness almost forces one to do so. One would no more choose to associate with 'first Christians' than one would with Polish Jews: not that one would need to prove so much as a single point against them. . . . Neither of them smell very pleasant. – I have looked in vain for so much as one sympathetic trait in the New Testament; there is nothing free, benevolent, open-hearted, honest in it. Humanity has not taken its first step here – the instincts of *cleanliness* are lacking. . . . There are only *bad* instincts in the New Testament, there is not even the courage for these bad instincts. Everything in it is cowardice, everything is self-deception and closing one's eyes to oneself. Every book becomes clean if one has just read the New Testament: to give an example, immediately after reading Paul I read with delight that sweetest and most high-spirited of all mockers, Petronius, of whom one could say what Domenico Boccaccio wrote to the Duke of Parma of Cesare Borgia: '*è tutto festo*' – immortally healthy, immortally cheerful and well-constituted. . . . For these little bigots miscalculate in the main thing. They attack, but everything attacked by them is thereby *signalized*. Whomever a 'first Christian' attacks is *not*

besmirched by it. ... Conversely: it is an honour to have
'first Christians' against one. It is impossible to read the New
Testament without feeling a partiality for that which is ill-
treated in it – to say nothing of the 'wisdom of this world'
which an impudent humbug tried in vain to confound. ...
But even the Scribes and Pharisees gain advantage from having such an opponent: they must have been worth something
to be hated in such an indecent fashion. Hypocrisy – that's
rich coming from 'first Christians'! – The Scribes and Pharisees were the *privileged*: this sufficed, Chandala hatred requires
no further reasons. The 'first Christian' – and, I fear, also the
'last Christian', *whom I shall perhaps live to see* – is a rebel in his
lowest instincts against everything privileged – he always lives
and struggles for '*equal rights*'. ... More closely considered,
he has no choice. If one wants to be, in one's own person,
'chosen of God' – or a 'temple of God', or a 'judge of angels'
– then every *other* principle of selection, for example on the
basis of integrity, intellect, manliness and pride, beauty and
liberality of heart, is simply 'world' – *evil as such*. ... Moral:
every word in the mouth of a 'first Christian' is a lie, every act
he performs an instinctive falsehood – all his values, all his
aims are harmful, but *whomever* he hates, *whatever* he hates, *has
value*. ... The Christian, the priestly Christian especially, is
a *criterion of values*. – Do I still have to add that in the entire New
Testament there is only *one* solitary figure one is obliged to
respect? Pilate, the Roman governor. To take a Jewish affair
seriously – he cannot persuade himself to do that. One Jew
more or less – what does it matter? ... The noble scorn of a
Roman before whom an impudent misuse of the word 'truth'
was carried on has enriched the New Testament with the only
expression *which possesses value* – which is its criticism, its
annihilation even: 'What is truth?' ...

47

– What sets *us* apart is not that we recognize no God, either in
history or in nature or behind nature – but that we find that
which has been reverenced as God not 'godlike' but pitiable,

absurd, harmful, not merely an error but a *crime against life.* . . .
We deny God as God. . . . If this God of the Christians were
proved to us to exist, we should know even less how to believe
in him. – In a formula: *Deus, qualem Paulus creavit, dei negatio.** –
A religion like Christianity, which is at no point in contact
with actuality, which crumbles away as soon as actuality
comes into its own at any point whatever, must naturally be a
mortal enemy of the 'wisdom of the world', that is to say of
science – it will approve of all expedients by which disciplining
of the intellect, clarity and severity in matters of intellectual
conscience, noble coolness and freedom of intellect, can be
poisoned and calumniated and *brought into ill repute.* 'Faith'
as an imperative is a *veto* against science – *in praxi* the lie at any
cost. . . . Paul *understood* the need for the lie, for 'faith'; the
Church subsequently understood Paul. – That God which
Paul invented for himself, a God who 'confounds the wisdom
of the world' (in a narrower sense the two great opponents
of all superstition, philology and medicine), is in reality only
the resolute *determination* of Paul himself to do so: to call one's
own will 'God', *Torah*† – that is quintessentially Jewish. Paul
wants to confound the 'wisdom of the world': his enemies are
the *good* philologists and physicians of the Alexandrian school
– upon them he makes war. In fact, one is not philologist and
physician without also being at the same time *anti-Christian.*
For as philologist one sees *behind* the 'sacred books', as physician *behind* the physiological depravity of the typical Christian.
The physician says 'incurable', the philologist 'fraud' . . .

48

– Has the famous story which stands at the beginning of the
Bible really been understood – the story of God's mortal
terror of *science*? . . . It has not been understood. This priest's-
book begins, as is only proper, with the priest's great inner
difficulty: *he* has only *one* great danger, *consequently* 'God' has
only *one* great danger. –

* God, as Paul created him, is a denial of God.
† 'The Law' in Paul's usage of the word.

The old God, all 'spirit', all high priest, all perfection, promenades in his garden: but he is bored. Against boredom the gods themselves fight in vain.* What does he do? He invents man – man is entertaining. . . . But behold, man too is bored. God's sympathy with the only kind of distress found in every Paradise knows no bounds: he forthwith creates other animals. God's *first* blunder: man did not find the animals entertaining – he dominated them, he did not even want to be an 'animal'. – Consequently God created woman. And then indeed there was an end to boredom – but also to something else! Woman was God's *second* blunder. – 'Woman is in her essence serpent, Heva' – every priest knows that; '*every* evil comes into the world through woman' – every priest knows that likewise. '*Consequently, science* too comes into the world through her'. . . . Only through woman did man learn to taste of the tree of knowledge. – What had happened? A mortal terror seized on the old God. Man himself had become God's *greatest* blunder; God had created for himself a rival, science makes *equal to God* – it is all over with priests and gods if man becomes scientific! – *Moral*: science is the forbidden in itself – it alone is forbidden. Science is the *first* sin, the germ of all sins, *original* sin. *This alone constitutes morality*. – 'Thou shalt *not* know' – the rest follows. – God's mortal terror did not stop him from being shrewd. How can one *defend* oneself against science? – that was for long his chief problem. Answer: away with man out of Paradise! Happiness, leisure gives room for thought – all thoughts are bad thoughts. . . . Man *shall* not think. – And the 'priest in himself' invents distress, death, the danger to life in pregnancy, every kind of misery, age, toil, above all *sickness* – nothing but expedients in the struggle against science! Distress does not *allow* man to think. . . . And nonetheless! oh horror! the structure of knowledge towers up, heaven-storming, reaching for the divine – what to do! – The old God invents *war*, he divides the peoples, he makes men destroy one another (– priests have always had need of war . . .). War – among other things a great mischief-maker in

* From a famous line in Schiller's *Maid of Orleans*: 'Against stupidity the gods themselves fight in vain.'

science! – Incredible! knowledge, *emancipation from the priest*, increases in spite of wars. – And the old God comes to a final decision: 'Man has become scientific – *there is nothing for it, he will have to be drowned!*' ...

49

– Have I been understood? The beginning of the Bible contains the *entire* psychology of the priest. – The priest knows only *one* great danger: that is science – the sound conception of cause and effect. But science flourishes in general only under happy circumstances – one must have a superfluity of time and intellect in order to 'know'. . . . '*Consequently* man must be made unhappy' – this has at all times been the logic of the priest. – One will already have guessed *what* only came into the world therewith, in accordance with this logic – 'sin'. . . . The concept of guilt and punishment, the entire 'moral world-order', was invented *in opposition to* science – *in opposition to* the detaching of man from the priest. . . . Man shall *not* look around him, he shall look down into himself; he shall *not* look prudently and cautiously into things in order to learn, he shall not look at all: he shall *suffer*. . . . And he shall suffer in such a way that he has need of the priest at all times. – Away with physicians! *One has need of a Saviour*. – The concept of guilt and punishment, including the doctrine of 'grace', of 'redemption', of 'forgiveness' – *lies* through and through and without any psychological reality – were invented to destroy the *causal sense* of man: they are an outrage on the concept cause and effect! – And *not* an outrage with the fist, with the knife, with honest hatred and love! But one from the most cowardly, cunning, lowest instincts! An *outrage of the priest!* An *outrage of the parasite!* A vampirism of pale subterranean bloodsuckers! . . . When the natural consequences of an act are no longer 'natural' but thought of as effected by the conceptual ghosts of superstition, by 'God', by 'spirits', by 'souls', as merely 'moral' consequences, as reward, punishment, sign, chastisement, then the precondition for knowledge has been destroyed – *then one has committed the greatest crime against humanity*. –

Sin, to say it again, that form *par excellence* of the self-violation of man, was invented to make science, culture, every kind of elevation and nobility of man impossible; the priest *rules* through the invention of sin. –

50

– At this point I cannot absolve myself from giving an account of the psychology of 'belief', of 'believers', for the use, as is only reasonable, of precisely the 'believers' themselves. If there is today still no lack of those who do not know how *indecent* it is to 'believe' – *or* a sign of *décadence*, of a broken will to live – well, they will know it tomorrow. My voice reaches even the hard-of-hearing. – It appears, if I have not misheard, that there exists among Christians a kind of criterion of truth called 'proof by potency'. 'Belief makes blessed: *therefore* it is true.' – One might here object straightaway that this making-blessed itself is not proved but only *promised*: blessedness conditional upon 'believing' – one *shall* become blessed *because* one believes. ... But *that* what the priest promises the believer for a 'Beyond' inaccessible to any control actually occurs, how could *that* be proved? – The alleged 'proof by potency' is therefore at bottom only a further belief that the effect which one promises oneself from the belief will not fail to appear. In a formula: 'I believe that belief makes blessed – consequently it is true'. – But with that we have already reached the end of the argument. This 'consequently' would be the *absurdum* itself as a criterion of truth. – But if, with no little indulgence, we suppose that the fact that belief makes blessed be regarded as proved (– *not* merely desired, *not* merely promised by the somewhat suspect mouth of a priest): would blessedness – more technically, *pleasure* – ever be a proof of truth? So little that it provides almost the counter-proof, at any rate the strongest suspicion against 'truth', when feelings of pleasure enter into the answer to the question 'what is true?' The proof by 'pleasure' is a proof *of* pleasure – that is all; when on earth was it established that *true* judgements give more enjoyment than false ones and, in accordance with a predetermined harmony, necessarily bring pleasant feelings in their train? – The experience of all severe, all profound intellects teaches *the reverse*. Truth has had to be fought for every step of the way, almost everything else dear to our hearts, on which our love and our trust in life depend, has had to be sacrificed to it. Greatness of soul is needed for it: the service of truth is the hardest service. – For what does it mean to be *honest* in intellectual things? That one is stern towards one's heart, that one despises 'fine feelings', that one makes every Yes and No a question of conscience! – Belief makes blessed: *consequently* it lies . . .

51

That under certain conditions belief makes blessed, that blessedness does not turn an *idée fixe* into a *true* idea, that faith moves no mountains but surely *places* mountains where there are none: a fleeting visit to a *madhouse* will provide ample enlightenment on these things. *Not*, I admit, to a priest: for he denies by instinct that sickness is sickness, that a madhouse is a madhouse. Christianity *needs* sickness almost as much as Hellenism needs a superfluity of health – *making* sick is the true hidden objective of the Church's whole system of salvation procedures. And the Church itself – is it not the Catholic madhouse as an ultimate ideal? – The whole earth as a madhouse? – The religious man as the Church *desires* him to be is a typical *décadent*; the moment when a religious crisis has gained the upper hand of a people is always characterized by epidemics of neurosis; the 'inner world' of the religious man is so like the 'inner world' of the over-excited and exhausted as to be mistaken for it; the 'highest' states which Christianity has hung up over mankind as the most valuable of all values are forms of epilepsy – the Church has canonized only lunatics or great imposters *in majorem dei honorem.** . . . I once permitted myself to describe the entire Christian penance-and-redemption training (which can be studied best today in England) as a methodically induced *folie circulaire*, naturally on a soil

* To the greater honour of God.

already prepared for it, that is to say a thoroughly morbid soil. No one is free to become a Christian or not to do so: one is not 'converted' to Christianity – one must be sufficiently sick for it. . . . We others, who have the *courage* for health *and* also for contempt, what contempt *we* have for a religion which teaches misunderstanding of the body! which does not wish to get rid of the soul-superstition! which makes a 'merit' of eating too little! which combats health as a kind of enemy, devil, temptation! which has persuaded itself that a 'perfect soul' could be carried about in a cadaver of a body and to do so needed to concoct a new conception of 'perfection', a pale, sickly, idiot-fanatic condition, so-called 'holiness' – holiness itself merely a symptom-syndrome of the impoverished, enervated, incurably corrupted body! . . . As a European movement, the Christian movement has been from the very first a collective movement of outcast and refuse elements of every kind (– these want to come to power through Christianity). It is *not* the expression of the decline of a race, it is an aggregate formation of *décadence* types from everywhere crowding together and seeking one another out. It is *not*, as is generally believed, the corruption of antiquity itself, of *noble* antiquity, which made Christianity possible: the learned idiocy which even today maintains such a thing cannot be contradicted too severely. The period in which the morbid, corrupt Chandala classes of the entire *Imperium* were becoming Christian was precisely that in which the *opposing type*, the nobility, existed in its fairest and maturest form. The majority became master; the democratism of the Christian instincts *conquered*. . . . Christianity was not 'national', not racially conditioned – it turned to the disinherited of life of every kind, it had its allies everywhere. Christianity has at its basis the *rancune* of the sick, the instinct directed *against* the healthy, *against* health. Everything well-constituted, proud, high-spirited, beauty above all, is hurtful to its ears and eyes. I recall again the invaluable saying of Paul: 'God hath chosen the *weak* things of the world, the *foolish* things of the world, *base* things of the world and things which are *despised*': *that* was the formula, *in hoc signo décadence* conquered. – *God on the Cross* – is the fearful hidden meaning behind this symbol still understood? – Everything that suffers, everything that hangs on the Cross, is *divine*. ... We all hang on the Cross, consequently *we* are divine. ... We alone are divine. ... Christianity was a victory, a *nobler* disposition perished by it – Christianity has been up till now mankind's greatest misfortune. –

52

Christianity also stands in opposition to all *intellectual* well-constitutedness – it *can* use only the morbid mind as the Christian mind, it takes the side of everything idiotic, it proclaims a curse against the 'spirit', against the *superbia* of the healthy spirit. Because sickness belongs to the essence of Christianity, the typical Christian condition, 'faith', *has* to be a form of sickness, every straightforward, honest, scientific road to knowledge *has* to be repudiated by the Church as a *forbidden* road. Even to doubt is a sin. ... The complete lack of psychological cleanliness in the priest – it betrays itself in his glance – is a consequent phenomenon of *décadence* – one can observe in hysterical women and rickety children how regularly instinctive falsity, lying for the sake of lying, inability to look straight and act straight, are expressions of *décadence*. 'Faith' means not *wanting* to know what is true. The pietist, the priest of both sexes, is false *because* he is sick: his instinct *demands* that truth shall not come into its own at any point. 'What makes sick is *good*; what proceeds from abundance, from superfluity, from power, is *evil*': that is what the believer feels. *Compulsion to lie* – in that I detect every predestined theologian. – Another mark of the theologian is his *incapacity for philology*. Philology is to be understood here in a very wide sense as the art of reading well – of being able to read off a fact *without* falsifying it by interpretation, *without* losing caution, patience, subtlety in the desire for understanding. Philology as *ephexis** in interpretation: whether it be a question of books, newspaper reports, fate or the weather – to say nothing of the 'salvation of the soul'. ... The way in which a

* undecisiveness.

theologian, no matter whether in Berlin or in Rome, interprets a 'word of the Scriptures', or an experience, a victory of his country's army for example, under the higher illumination of the psalms of David, is always so *audacious* as to make a philologist run up every wall in sight. And what on earth is he to do when pietists and other cows out of Swabia dress up the pathetic commonplace and stuffiness of their existence with the 'finger of God' into a miracle of 'grace', of 'divine providence', of 'experience of salvation'! Yet the most modest expenditure of intelligence, not to say *decency*, would convince these interpreters of the complete childishness and unworthiness of such an abuse of divine dexterity.* Even the slightest trace of piety in us ought to make us feel that a God who cures a headcold at the right moment or tells us to get into a coach just as a downpour is about to start is so absurd a God he would have to be abolished even if he existed. A God as a domestic servant, as a postman, as an almanac-maker – at bottom a word for the stupidest kind of accidental occurrence. ... 'Divine providence', as it is still believed in today by almost every third person in 'cultured Germany', would be a stronger objection to God than any other that could possibly be thought of. And in any case it is an objection to the Germans! ...

53

– That *martyrs* prove anything about the truth of a cause is so little true I would be disposed to deny that a martyr has ever had anything whatever to do with truth. In the tone with which a martyr throws his opinion at the world's head there is already expressed so low a degree of intellectual integrity, such *obtuseness* to the question of 'truth', that one never needs to refute a martyr. Truth is not something one person might possess and another not possess: peasants at the most, or peasant apostles like Luther, could think of truth in this fashion. One may be certain that modesty, *moderation* in intellectual matters, increases with the degree of conscientiousness in them. To *know* five things and gently decline to

* *'Fingerfertigkeit'* plays upon 'finger of God'.

know anything *else*. ... 'Truth' as every prophet, every sectarian, every latitudinarian, every Socialist, every Churchman understands the word, is conclusive proof that not so much as a start has been made on that disciplining of the intellect and self-overcoming necessary for the discovery of any truth, even the very smallest. – Martyrdoms, by the way, have been a great misfortune in history: they have *seduced*. ... The inference of all idiots, women and nations included, that a cause for which someone is willing to die (not to speak of those which, like primitive Christianity, produce epidemics of death-seeking) must have something in it – this inference has become an unspeakable drag on verification, on the spirit of verification and caution. Martyrs have *harmed* truth. ... And even today a crude sort of persecution is all that is required to create an *honourable* name for any sect, no matter how indifferent in itself. – What? does the fact that someone gives up his life for it change anything in the value of a cause? – An error which becomes honourable is an error which possesses one seductive charm more: do you believe, *messieurs* the theologians, that we would give you an opportunity of becoming martyrs for your lies? – one refutes a thing by laying it respectfully on ice – just so does one refute theologians too. ... The world-historical stupidity of all persecutors has lain precisely in giving their opponents the appearance of honourableness – in bestowing on them the fascination of martyrdom. ... Woman is today on her knees before an error because she has been told someone died on the Cross for it. *Is the Cross then an argument?* – But on all these things one man alone has said the word that has been wanting for millennia – *Zarathustra*.

They wrote letters of blood on the path they followed and their folly taught that truth is proved by blood.

But blood is the worst witness of truth; blood poisons and transforms the purest teaching to delusion and hatred of the heart.

And if someone goes through fire for his teaching – what does that prove? Truly, it is more when one's own teaching comes out of one's own burning!*

* *Thus Spoke Zarathustra,* Part III, 'Of the Priests'.

54

One should not let oneself be misled: great intellects are sceptics. Zarathustra is a sceptic. The vigour of a mind, its *freedom* through strength and superior strength, is *proved* by scepticism. Men of conviction simply do not come into consideration where the fundamentals of value and disvalue are concerned. Convictions are prisons. They do not see far enough, they do not see things *beneath* them: but to be permitted to speak about value and disvalue one must see five hundred convictions *beneath* one – *behind* one. . . . A spirit which wants to do great things, which also wills the means for it, is necessarily a sceptic. Freedom from convictions of any kind, the *capacity* for an unconstrained view, *pertains* to strength. . . . Grand passion, the ground and force of his being, even more enlightened, more despotic than he himself is, takes his whole intellect into its service; it makes him intrepid; it even gives him the courage for unholy means; if need be it *permits* him convictions. Conviction as a *means*: there is much one can achieve only by means of a conviction. Grand passion uses and uses up convictions, it does not submit to them – it knows itself sovereign. – Conversely: the need for belief, for some unconditional Yes and No, Carlylism if I may be excused the expression, is a requirement of *weakness*. The man of faith, the 'believer' of every sort is necessarily a dependent man – such as cannot out of himself posit ends at all. The 'believer' does not belong to *himself*, he can be only a means, he has to be *used*, he needs someone who will use him. His instinct accords the highest honour to a morality of selflessness: everything persuades him to it, his intelligence, his experience, his vanity. Belief of any kind is itself an expression of selflessness, of self-alienation. . . . If one considers what need people have of an external regulation to constrain and steady them, how compulsion, *slavery* in a higher sense, is the sole and final condition under which the person of weaker will, woman especially, can prosper: then one also understands the nature of conviction, 'faith'. Conviction is the backbone of the man of conviction. *Not* to see many things, not to be impartial in anything, to be party through and through, to view all values from a strict and necessary perspective – this alone is the condition under which such a man exists at all. But he is thereby the antithesis, the *antagonist* of the truthful man – of truth. . . . The believer is not free to have a conscience at all over the question 'true' and 'false': to be honest on *this* point would mean his immediate destruction. The pathological conditionality of his perspective makes of the convinced man a fanatic – Savonarola, Luther, Rousseau, Robespierre, Saint-Simon – the antithetical type of the strong, emancipated spirit. But the larger-than-life attitudes of these *sick* spirits, these conceptual epileptics, impresses the great masses – fanatics are picturesque, mankind would rather see gestures than listen to *reasons* . . .

55

– A further step in the psychology of conviction, of 'belief'. I suggested long ago that convictions might be more dangerous enemies of truth than lies. This time I should like to pose the decisive question: is there any difference whatever between a lie and a conviction? – All the world believes there is, but what does all the world not believe! – Every conviction has its history, its preliminary forms, its tentative shapes, its blunders: it *becomes* a conviction after *not* being one for a long time, after *hardly* being one for an even longer time. What? could the lie not be among these embryonic forms of conviction? – Sometimes it requires merely a change in persons: in the son that becomes conviction which in the father was still a lie. – I call a lie: wanting *not* to see something one does see, wanting not to see something *as* one sees it: whether the lie takes place before witnesses or without witnesses is of no consequence. The most common lie is the lie one tells to oneself; lying to others is relatively the exception. – Now this desiring *not* to see what one sees, this desiring not to see as one sees, is virtually the primary condition for all who are in any sense *party*: the party man necessarily becomes a liar. German historiography, for example, is convinced that Rome was despotism, that the Teutons brought the spirit of freedom into the world: what difference is there between this conviction and a lie? Is there any further need to be surprised if all parties, German historians included, instinctively have the big moral words in their mouths – that morality *continues to exist* virtually because the party man of every sort has need of it every moment? – 'This is *our* conviction: we confess it before all the world, we live and die for it – respect everything that has convictions!' – I have heard this kind of thing even from the lips of anti-Semites. On the contrary, gentlemen! An anti-Semite is certainly not made more decent by the fact that he lies on principle. . . . The priests, who are subtler in such things and understand very well the objection that can be raised to the concept of a conviction, that is to say mendaciousness on principle *because* serving a purpose, have taken over from the Jews the prudence of inserting the concept 'God', 'the will of God', 'the revelation of God' in its place. Kant too, with his categorical imperative, was on the same road: his reason became *practical* in this matter. – There are questions whose truth or untruth *cannot* be decided by man; all the supreme questions, all the supreme problems of value are beyond human reason. . . . To grasp the limits of reason – only *this* is truly philosophy. . . . To what end did God give mankind revelation? Would God have done anything superfluous? Mankind *cannot* of itself know what is good and what evil, therefore God taught mankind his will. . . . Moral: the priest does *not* lie – the question 'true' or 'untrue' does not *arise* in such things as priests speak of; these things do not permit of lying at all. For in order to lie one would have to be able to decide *what* is true here. But this is precisely what mankind *cannot* do; the priest is thus only God's mouthpiece. – This kind of priestly syllogism is by no means only Jewish and Christian; the right to lie and the *shrewdness* of a 'revelation' pertains to the type priest, to priests of *décadence* as much as to priests of paganism (– pagans are all who say Yes to life, to whom 'God' is the word for the great Yes to all things). – The 'Law', the 'will of God', the 'sacred book', 'inspiration' – all merely words for the conditions *under* which the priest comes to power, *by* which he maintains his power – these concepts are to be found at the basis of all priestly organizations, all priestly or priestly-philosophical power-structures. The 'holy lie' – common to Confucius, the Law-Book of Manu, Moham-med, the Christian Church – : it is not lacking in Plato. 'The truth exists': this means, wherever it is heard, *the priest is lying* . . .

56

– Ultimately the point is to what *end* a lie is told. That 'holy' ends are lacking in Christianity is *my* objection to its means. Only *bad* ends: the poisoning, slandering, denying of life, contempt for the body, the denigration and self-violation of man through the concept sin – *consequently* its means too are bad. – It is with an opposite feeling that I read the Law-Book of *Manu*, an incomparably spiritual and superior work, so much as to *name* which in the same breath as the Bible would be a sin against the *spirit*. One sees immediately that it has a real philosophy behind it, *in* it, not merely an ill-smelling Jewish acidity compounded of rabbinism and superstition – it gives even the most fastidious psychologist something to bite on. *Not* forgetting the main thing, *the* basic difference from any sort of Bible: it is the means by which the *noble* orders, the philosophers and the warriors, keep the mob under control; noble values everywhere, a feeling of perfection, an affirmation of life, a triumphant feeling of well-being in oneself and of goodwill towards life – the *sun* shines on the entire book. – All the things upon which Christianity vents its abysmal vulgarity, procreation for example, woman, marriage, are here treated seriously, with reverence, with love and trust. How can one actually put into the hands of women and children a book containing the low-minded saying: 'To avoid fornication let every man have his own wife, and let every woman have her own husband . . . for it is better to marry than burn'?* And is it *allowable* to be a Christian as long as the origin of man is Christianized, that is to say *dirtied*, with the concept of the

* 1 Corinthians vii , 2 and 9.

immaculata conceptio? . . . I know of no book in which so many tender and kind remarks are addressed to woman as in the Law-Book of Manu; these old greybeards and saints have a way of being polite to women which has perhaps never been surpassed. 'A woman's mouth' – it says in one place – 'a girl's breast, a child's prayer, the smoke of a sacrifice are always pure'. Another passage: 'There is nothing purer than the light of the sun, the shadow of a cow, air, water, fire and a girl's breath.' A final passage – perhaps also a holy lie – : 'All the openings of the body above the navel are pure, all below impure. Only in the case of a girl is the whole body pure.'

57

One catches the *unholiness* of the Christian means *in flagranti* when one compares the *Christian* purpose with the purpose of the Manu Law-Book – when one throws a bright light on this greatest of antitheses of purpose. The critic of Christianity cannot be spared the task of making Christianity *contemptible*. – Such a law-book as that of Manu originates as does every good law-book: it summarizes the experience, policy and experimental morality of long centuries, it settles accounts, it creates nothing new. The precondition for a codification of this sort is the insight that the means of endowing with authority a *truth* slowly and expensively acquired are fundamentally different from those by which one would demonstrate it. A law-book never tells of the utility of a law, of the reason for it, of the casuistry which preceded it: for in that way it would lose the imperative tone, the 'thou shalt', the precondition of being obeyed. The problem lies precisely in this. – At a certain point in the evolution of a people its most enlightened, that is to say most reflective and far-sighted, class declares the experience in accordance with which the people is to live – that is, *can* live – to be fixed and settled. Their objective is to bring home the richest and completest harvest from the ages of experimentation and *bad* experience. What, consequently, is to be prevented above all is the continuation of experimenting, the perpetuation *in infinitum* of the fluid condition of values, tests, choices, criticizing of values. A two-fold wall is erected against this: firstly *revelation*, that is the assertion that the reason for these laws is *not* of human origin, was *not* sought and found slowly and with many blunders, but, being of divine origin, is whole, perfect, without history, a gift, a miracle, merely communicated. . . . Then *tradition*, that is, the assertion that the law has already existed from time immemorial, that it is impious, a crime against the ancestors, to call it in question. The authority of the law is established by the thesis: God *gave* it, the ancestors *lived* it. – The higher rationale of such a procedure lies in the intention of gradually making the way of life recognized as correct (that is *demonstrated* by a tremendous amount of finely-sifted experience) unconscious: so that a complete automatism of instinct is achieved – the precondition for any kind of mastery, any kind of perfection in the art of living. To set up a law-book of the kind of Manu means to concede to a people the right henceforth to become masterly, to become perfect – to be ambitious for the highest art of living. *To that end the law must be made unconscious:* this is the purpose of every holy lie. – The *order of castes*, the supreme, the dominating law, is only the sanctioning of a *natural order*, a natural law of the first rank over which no arbitrary caprice, no 'modern idea' has any power. In every healthy society, there can be distinguished three types of man of divergent physiological tendency which mutually condition one another and each of which possesses its own hygiene, its own realm of work, its own sort of mastery and feeling of perfection. Nature, *not* Manu, separates from one another the predominantly spiritual type, the predominantly muscular and temperamental type, and the third type distinguished neither in the one nor the other, the mediocre type – the last as the great majority, the first as the elite. The highest caste – I call it *the very few* – possesses, as the perfect caste, also the privileges of the very few: among them is that of representing happiness, beauty, benevolence on earth. Only the most spiritual human beings are permitted beauty, beautiful things: only in their case is benevolence not weakness. *Pulchrum est paucorum hominum:* the good is a privilege. On the other hand, nothing is more strictly forbidden them than ugly manners or a pessimistic outlook, an eye that *makes ugly* – to say nothing of indignation at the collective aspect of things. Indignation is the privilege of the Chandala; pessimism likewise. '*The world is perfect*' – thus speaks the instinct of the most spiritual, the affirmative instinct – : 'imperfection, everything *beneath* us, distance between man and man, the pathos of this distance, the Chandala themselves pertain to this perfection'. The most spiritual human beings, as the *strongest*, find their happiness where others would find their destruction: in the labyrinth, in severity towards themselves and others, in attempting; their joy lies in self-constraint: with them asceticism becomes nature, need, instinct. They consider the hard task a privilege, to play with vices which overwhelm others a *recreation*. . . . Knowledge – a form of asceticism. – They are the most venerable kind of human being: this does not exclude their being the most cheerful, the most amiable. They rule not because they want to but because they *are*; they are not free to be second in rank. – The *second* in rank: these are the guardians of the law, the keepers of order and security; the noble warriors; above all the *king* as the highest formula of warrior, judge and upholder of the law. The second in rank are the executives of the most spiritual order, the closest to them who relieve them of everything *coarse* in the work of ruling – their following, their right hand, their best pupils. – In all this, to say it again, there is nothing capricious, nothing 'artificial'; whatever is *different* from this is artificial – nature is then confounded. . . . The order of castes, *order of rank*, only formulates the supreme law of life itself; the separation of the three types is necessary for the preservation of society, for making possible higher and higher types – *inequality* of rights is the condition for the existence of rights at all. – A right is a privilege. The privilege of each is determined by the nature of his being. Let us not underestimate the privileges of the *mediocre*. Life becomes harder and harder as it approaches the *heights* – the coldness increases, the responsibility increases. A high culture is a pyramid: it can stand only on a broad base, its very first prerequisite is a strongly and soundly consolidated mediocrity. The crafts, trade, agriculture, *science*, the greater part of art, in a word the entire compass of *professional* activity, are in no way compatible with anything other than mediocrity in ability and desires; these things would be out of place among the elite, the instinct pertaining to them is as much opposed to aristocracy as it is to anarchy. To be a public utility, a cog, a function, is a natural vocation: it is *not* society, it is the kind of *happiness* of which the great majority are alone capable, which makes intelligent machines of them. For the mediocre it is happiness to be mediocre; mastery in one thing, specialization, is for them a natural instinct. It would be quite unworthy of a more profound mind to see an objection in mediocrity as such. It is even the *prime* require-ment for the existence of exceptions: a high culture is con-ditional upon it. When an exceptional human being handles the mediocre more gently than he does himself or his equals, this is not mere politeness of the heart* – it is simply his *duty*. . . . Whom among today's rabble do I hate the most? The Socialist rabble, the Chandala apostles who undermine the worker's instinct, his pleasure, his feeling of contentment with his little state of being – who make him envious, who teach him revengefulness. . . . Injustice never lies in unequal rights, it lies in the claim to '*equal*' rights. . . . What is *bad*? But I have already answered that question: everything that proceeds from weakness, from envy, from *revengefulness*. – The anarchist and the Christian have a common origin . . .

58

It does indeed make a difference for what purpose one lies: whether one preserves with a lie or *destroys* with it. One may assert an absolute equivalence between *Christian* and *anarchist*: their purpose, their instinct is set only on destruction. For the proof of this proposition one has only to read history, which displays it with frightful clarity. If we have just now examined a religious legislation the purpose of which was to 'eternalize'

* A phrase from Goethe's *Elective Affinities*.

a grand organization of society, the supreme condition for the *prosperity* of life – Christianity discovered its mission in making an end of just such an organization *because life prospered within it*. There the revenue of reason from long ages of experimentation and uncertainty was to be employed for the benefit of the most distant future and the biggest, richest, most complete harvest possible brought home: here, on the contrary, the harvest was *poisoned* overnight. ... That which stood *aere perennius*, the *Imperium Romanum*, the most grandiose form of organization under difficult conditions which has hitherto been achieved, in comparison with which everything before and everything since is patchwork, bungling, dilettantism – these holy anarchists made it an 'act of piety' to destroy 'the world', that is to say the *Imperium Romanum*, until not one stone was left standing on another – until even Teutons and other such ruffians could become master of it. ... The Christian and the anarchist: both *décadents*, both incapable of producing anything but dissolution, poisoning, degeneration, both *bloodsuckers*, both with the instinct of *deadly hatred* towards everything that stands erect, that towers grandly up, that possesses duration, that promises life a future. ... Christianity was the vampire of the *Imperium Romanum* – the tremendous deed of the Romans in clearing the ground for a great culture *which could take its time* was undone overnight by Christianity. – Is this still not understood? The *Imperium Romanum* which we know, which the history of the Roman province teaches us to know better and better, this most admirable of all works of art in the grand style, was a beginning, its structure was calculated to *prove* itself by millennia – to this day there has never been such building, to build in such a manner *sub specie aeterni* has never been so much as dreamed of! – This organization was firm enough to endure bad emperors: the accident of persons must have no effect on such things – *first* principle of all grand architecture. But it was not firm enough to endure the *corruptest* form of corruption, to endure the *Christian*. ... These stealthy vermin which, shrouded in night, fog and ambiguity crept up to every individual and sucked seriousness for *real* things, the instinct for *realities* of any kind, out of him, this cowardly, womanish and honeyed crew gradually alienated the 'souls' of this tremendous structure – those precious, those manly-noble natures who found their own cause, their own seriousness, their own pride in the cause of Rome. This underhanded bigotry, conventicle secrecy, gloomy concepts such as Hell, such as the sacrifice of the innocent, such as the *unio mystica* in blood-drinking, above all the slowly stirred-up fire of revengefulness, of Chandala revengefulness – *that* is what became master of Rome, the same species of religion on whose antecedent form Epicurus had already made war. One must read Lucretius to understand *what* it was Epicurus opposed: *not* paganism but 'Christianity', which is to say the corruption of souls through the concept of guilt, punishment and immortality. – He opposed the subterranean cults, the whole of latent Christianity – to deny immortality was already in those days a real *redemption*. – And Epicurus would have won, every mind of any account in the Roman Empire was an Epicurean: *then Paul appeared.* . . . Paul, Chandala hatred against Rome, against 'the world', become flesh and genius, the Jew, the *eternal* Jew* par excellence. . . . What he divined was that with the aid of the little sectarian movement on the edge of Judaism one could ignite a 'world conflagration', that with the symbol 'God on the Cross' one could sum up everything down-trodden, everything in secret revolt, the entire heritage of anarchist agitation in the Empire into a tremendous power. 'Salvation is of the Jews.' – Christianity as the formula for outbidding all the subterranean cults, those of Osiris, of the Great Mother, of Mithras for example – *and* for summing them up: it is in this insight that the genius of Paul consists. His instinct in this matter was so sure that, doing ruthless violence to the truth, he took the ideas by which those Chandala religions exercised their fascination and placed them in the mouth of the 'Saviour' he had invented, and not only in his mouth – so as to *make* of him something even a priest of Mithras could understand. . . . This was his vision on the road to Damascus: he grasped that to disvalue 'the world' he *needed* the belief in immortality, that the concept 'Hell' will

* 'The eternal Jew' is also the German form of the Wandering Jew.

master even Rome – that with the 'Beyond' one *kills life*. . . .
Nihilist and Christian: they rhyme,* and do not merely
rhyme . . .

59

The whole labour of the ancient world *in vain*: I have no words
to express my feelings at something so dreadful. – And considering its labour was a preparation, that only the substruc-
ture for a labour of millennia had, with granite self-confidence,
been laid, the whole *meaning* of the ancient world in vain! . . .
Why did the Greeks exist? Why the Romans? – Every prerequisite for an erudite culture, all the scientific *methods* were
already there, the great, the incomparable art of reading well
had already been established – the prerequisite for a cultural
tradition, for a uniform science; natural science, in concert
with mathematics and mechanics, was on the best possible
road – the *sense for facts*, the last-developed and most valuable
of all the senses, had its schools and its tradition already centuries old! Is this understood? Everything *essential* for setting
to work had been devised – methods, one must repeat ten
times, *are* the essential, as well as being the most difficult, as
well as being that which has habit and laziness against it
longest. What we have won back for ourselves today with an
unspeakable amount of self-constraint – for we all still have
bad instincts, the Christian instincts, somewhere within us –
the free view of reality, the cautious hand, patience and seriousness in the smallest things, the whole *integrity* of knowledge –
was already there! already more than two millennia ago! *And*
good and delicate taste and tact! *Not* as brain training! *Not*
as 'German' culture with the manners of ruffians! But as
body, as gesture, as instinct – in a word, as reality. . . . *All in
vain!* Overnight merely a memory! – Greeks! Romans!
nobility of instinct, of taste, methodical investigation, genius
for organization and government, the faith in, the *will* to a
future for mankind, the great Yes to all things, visibly present
to all the senses as the *Imperium Romanum*, grand style no
longer merely art but become reality, truth, *life*. . . . And not

* In German, *Nihilist und Christ* do rhyme.

overwhelmed overnight by a natural event! Not trampled
down by Teutons and other such clodhoppers! But ruined by
cunning, secret, invisible, anaemic vampires! Not conquered –
only sucked dry! ... Covert revengefulness, petty envy
become *master!* Everything pitiful, everything suffering from
itself, everything tormented by base feelings, the whole
ghetto-world of the soul suddenly *on top!* – One has only to read
any of the Christian agitators, Saint Augustine for example, to
realize, to *smell*, what dirty fellows had therewith come out on
top. One would be deceiving oneself utterly if one presupposed
a lack of intelligence of any sort on the part of the leaders of
the Christian movement – oh they are shrewd, shrewd to the
point of holiness, these Church Fathers! What they lack is
something quite different. Nature was neglectful when she
made them – she forgot to endow them with even a modest
number of respectable, decent, *cleanly* instincts. ... Between
ourselves, they are not even men. ... If Islam despises
Christianity, it is a thousand times right to do so: Islam presupposes *men* ...

60

Christianity robbed us of the harvest of the culture of the
ancient world, it later went on to rob us of the harvest of the
culture of *Islam*. The wonderful Moorish cultural world of
Spain, more closely related to *us* at bottom, speaking more
directly to our senses and taste, than Greece and Rome, was
trampled down (– I do not say by what kind of feet –): why?
because it was noble, because it owed its origin to manly
instincts, because it said Yes to life even in the rare and ex-
quisite treasures of Moorish life! ... Later on, the Crusaders
fought against something they would have done better to lie
down in the dust before – a culture compared with which
even our nineteenth century may well think itself very impoverished and very 'late'. – They wanted booty, to be sure:
the Orient was rich. ... But let us not be prejudiced! The
Crusades – higher piracy, that is all! German knighthood,
Viking knighthood at bottom, was there in its element: the
Church knew only too well what German knighthood can be

had for. . . . The German knights, always the 'Switzers' of the Church, always in the service of all the bad instincts of the Church – but *well paid*. . . . That it is precisely with the aid of German swords, German blood and courage, that the Church has carried on its deadly war against everything noble on earth! A host of painful questions arise at this point. The German aristocracy is virtually *missing* in the history of higher culture: one can guess the reason. . . . Christianity, alcohol – the two *great* means of corruption. . . . For in itself there should be no choice in the matter when faced with Islam and Christianity, as little as there should when faced with an Arab and a Jew. The decision is given in advance; no one is free to choose here. One either *is* Chandala or one is *not*. . . . 'War to the knife with Rome! Peace, friendship with Islam': this is what that great free spirit, the genius among German emperors, Friedrich the Second, felt, this is what he *did*. What? does a German have to be a genius, a free spirit, before he can have *decent* feelings? How a German could ever have felt *Christian* escapes me . . .

61

Here it is necessary to touch on a memory a hundred times more painful for Germans. The Germans have robbed Europe of the last great cultural harvest Europe had to bring home – of the harvest of *Renaissance*. Is it at last understood, is there a *desire* to understand, *what* the Renaissance was? The *revaluation of Christian values*, the attempt, undertaken with every expedient, with every instinct, with genius of every kind, to bring about the victory of the opposing values, the *noble* values. . . . Up till now *this* has been the only great war, there has been no more decisive interrogation than that conducted by the Renaissance – the question it asks is the question *I* ask – : neither has there been a form of *attack* more fundamental, more direct, and more strenuously delivered on the entire front and at the enemy's centre! To attack at the decisive point, in the very seat of Christianity, to set the *noble* values on the throne, which is to say to set them *into* the instincts, the deepest needs and desires of him who sits thereon. . . . I see in my mind's eye a *possibility* of a quite unearthly fascination and splendour – it seems to glitter with a trembling of every refinement of beauty, there seems to be at work in it an art so divine, so diabolically divine, that one might scour the millennia in vain for a second such possibility; I behold a spectacle at once so meaningful and so strangely paradoxical it would have given all the gods of Olympus an opportunity for an immortal roar of laughter – *Cesare Borgia as Pope*. . . . Am I understood? . . . Very well, *that* would have been a victory of the only sort *I* desire today – : Christianity would thereby have been *abolished*! – What happened? A German monk, Luther, went to Rome. This monk, all the vindictive instincts of a failed priest in him, fulminated in Rome *against* the Renaissance. . . . Instead of grasping with profound gratitude the tremendous event which had taken place, the overcoming of Christianity in its very *seat* – his hatred grasped only how to nourish itself on this spectacle. The religious man thinks only of himself. – What Luther saw was the *corruption* of the Papacy, while precisely the opposite was palpably obvious: the old corruption, the *peccatum originale*, Christianity *no* longer sat on the Papal throne! Life sat there instead! the triumph of life! the great Yes to all lofty, beautiful, daring things! . . . And Luther *restored the Church:* he attacked it. . . . The Renaissance – an event without meaning, a great *in vain*! – Oh these Germans, what they have already cost us! In vain – that has always been the *work* of the Germans. – The Reformation; Leibniz; Kant and so-called German philosophy; the Wars of 'Liberation'; the *Reich* – each time an in vain for something already in existence, for something *irretrievable*. . . . They are *my* enemies, I confess it, these Germans: I despise in them every kind of uncleanliness of concept and value, of *cowardice* in the face of every honest Yes and No. For almost a millennium they have twisted and tangled everything they have laid their hands on, they have on their conscience all the half-heartedness – three-eighths-heartedness! – from which Europe is sick – they also have on their conscience the uncleanest kind of Christianity there is, the most incurable kind, the kind hardest to refute,

Protestantism. . . . If we never get rid of Christianity, the *Germans* will be to blame . . .

62

– With that I have done and pronounce my judgement. I *condemn* Christianity, I bring against the Christian Church the most terrible charge any prosecutor has ever uttered. To me it is the extremest thinkable form of corruption, it has had the will to the ultimate corruption conceivably possible. The Christian Church has left nothing untouched by its depravity, it has made of every value a disvalue, of every truth a lie, of every kind of integrity a vileness of soul. People still dare to talk to me of its 'humanitarian' blessings! To *abolish* any state of distress whatever has been profoundly inexpedient to it: it has lived on states of distress, it has *created* states of distress in order to eternalize *itself*. . . . The worm of sin, for example: it was only the Church which enriched mankind with this state of distress! – 'Equality of souls before God', this false-hood, this *pretext* for the *rancune* of all the base-minded, this explosive concept which finally became revolution, modern idea and the principle of the decline of the entire social order – is *Christian* dynamite. . . . 'Humanitarian' blessings of Christianity! To cultivate out of *humanitas* a self-contradiction, an art of self-violation, a will to falsehood at any price, an antipathy, a contempt for every good and honest instinct! These are the blessings of Christianity! – Parasitism as the *sole* practice of the Church; with its ideal of green-sickness, of 'holiness' draining away all blood, all love, all hope for life; the Beyond as the will to deny reality of every kind; the Cross as the badge of recognition for the most subterranean conspiracy there has ever been – a conspiracy against health, beauty, well-constitutedness, bravery, intellect, *benevolence* of soul, *against life itself* . . .

Wherever there are walls I shall inscribe this eternal accusation against Christianity upon them – I can write in letters which make even the blind see. . . . I call Christianity the *one* great curse, the *one* great intrinsic depravity, the *one* great instinct for revenge for which no expedient is sufficiently poisonous, secret, subterranean, *petty* – I call it the *one* immortal blemish of mankind . . .

And one calculates *time* from the *dies nefastus** on which this fatality arose – from the *first* day of Christianity! – *Why not rather from its last? – From today?* – Revaluation of all values!

* unlucky day.

APPENDICES

A

Nietzsche disparages philosophical systems from the side of him who invents them and from that of him who is influenced – 'seduced' – by them. He thinks the former should realize that no system can be 'true' because it must ultimately depend upon some unproven assumption originating in the personality of its maker. 'In every philosophy there is a point at which the "conviction" of the philosopher steps upon the scene . . .' (*Beyond Good and Evil* 8) and if this 'conviction' is the basis of a 'system' it vitiates the system. Refusal to question this conviction, assumption, is in a philosopher dishonesty: 'the will to a system is a lack of integrity.' (For a criticism of system-philosophy as the prisoner of its own grammar see Appendix C.) To illustrate Nietzsche's objection to systems from the point of view of those who fall under their influence it will be useful to quote aphorism 31 of *Assorted Opinions and Maxims* (1879), since this will also provide an example of the style of extended conceit which even at this relatively late date Nietzsche still thought effective and the compression of which into the metaphorical style represented by the foreword to *The Anti-Christ* is one of his greatest achievements as a prose writer (an evolution comparable with Shakespeare's or with the development of English 'poetic logic' – George Ryland's term – from *Euphues* to the characteristic metaphors of Shelley):

In the desert of science. – To the man of science on his unassuming and laborious travels, which must often enough be journeys through the desert, there appear those glittering mirages called 'philosophical systems': with bewitching deceptive power they show the solution of all enigmas and the freshest draught of the true water of life to be near at hand; his heart rejoices, and it seems to the weary traveller that his lips already touch the goal of all the perseverance and sorrows of the scientific life, so that he involuntarily presses forward. There are other natures, to be sure, which stand still, as if bewildered by the fair illusion: the desert swallows them up and they are dead to science. Other natures again, which have often before experienced this subjective solace, may well grow exceedingly ill-humoured and curse the salty taste which these apparitions leave behind in the mouth and from which arises a raging thirst – without one having been brought so much as a single step nearer to any kind of spring.

B

It is consistent with the whole cast of Nietzsche's thought that he should see in logic an instrument and not something possessing validity independent of the use to which it is intended to be put. I think it is fair to say that he adopts this attitude towards everything with which he deals: hence the indispensability, to himself most of all, of his concept of the 'will to power' – it provides *that which uses*. Apparent inconsistencies in his work can often be explained by understanding whether he is speaking of a thing as it is generally taken to be or from the point of view of the will to power: thus he can both deny that a 'system of conventional signs such as constitutes logic' is of any value whatever and affirm the value of logic as an instrument. The negative side of this judgement appears in such formulations as this from *Human, All Too Human* (1878), aphorism 11:

... *logic* rests on presuppositions with which nothing in the actual world corresponds, for example on the presupposition that there are equivalent things, that a thing is identical at different points of time. ... It is the same with *mathematics*, which would certainly have not come into existence if one had known from the beginning that there was in nature no exactly straight line, no actual circle, no absolute magnitude.

The positive side appears after the introduction of the hypothesis of a will to power (in the first part of *Thus Spoke Zarathustra*, 1883), as in aphorism 3 of *Beyond Good and Evil* (1886):

... behind all logic ... there stand evaluations, in plainer terms physiological demands, for the preservation of a definite species of life. For example, that the definite shall be of greater value than the indefinite, appearance of less value than 'truth': but such valuations as these could, their regulatory importance for *us* notwithstanding, be no more than foreground valuations, a definite species of *niaiserie* [foolishness] which may be necessary precisely for the preservation of beings like us. Assuming, that is, that it is not precisely man who is the 'measure of things' . . .

Finally, among many notes of a similar tendency published in *The Will to Power* we find:

Towards an understanding of logic: *the will to make equivalent is the will to power* . . . (511, written 1885–6).

In the 1887 edition of *The Gay Science* (aphorism 370) Nietzsche defines logic as 'the abstract intelligibility of existence'; re-printing this definition in *Nietzsche contra Wagner* (1888) he adds the words 'even for idiots'.

C

The hyperbolic formulation 'I fear we are not getting rid of God because we still believe in grammar' has its prehistory in Nietzsche's long insistence that words give us the illusion that we have described something or discovered some truth about it when we have merely named it, and the further illusion that the existence of a word guarantees the existence of whatever the word refers to. Because the grammar of the language we have inherited is founded upon a relationship between subject and predicate, we cannot help thinking this subject-predicate relationship into the real world in the form of 'thing' and the 'action' of a thing, of 'being' and 'doing'; ultimately we believe in 'God-world' only because we believe in 'subject-predicate'. Three brief examples of Nietzsche's thinking on this topic:

The significance of language for the evolution of culture resides in the fact that in language man set a world of his own over against the other world. . . . To the extent that man has for long ages believed in the concepts and names of things as in *aeternae veritates* [eternal truths] he has appropriated to himself that pride by which

he raised himself above the animal: he really thought that in language he possessed knowledge of the world. The sculptor of language
was not so modest as to believe that he was only giving things
designations, he conceived rather that with words he was expressing supreme knowledge of things: language is, in fact, the first stage
of the occupation with science . . . (*Human, All Too Human* 11.)

Discussing the human habit of collecting phenomena together
in a group and isolating this aggregate as a 'fact':

The word and the concept are the most obvious reason why we
believe in this isolation of groups of actions: we do not merely
designate things by them, we originally believe that through them
we grasp what is *true* in things. Through words and concepts we
are now continually tempted to think of things as being simpler than
they are, as separated from one another, as indivisible, each existing
in and for itself. There is a philosophical mythology concealed in
language . . . (*The Wanderer and his Shadow* [1880] 11.)

Individual philosophical ideas are not arbitrary but belong to a
system of thinking in the same way as the limbs of an animal
belong together:

The singular family resemblance between all Indian, Greek and
German philosophizing is easy enough to explain. Where, thanks to
the common philosophy of grammar – I mean thanks to unconscious domination and directing by similar grammatical functions
– there exists a language affinity it is quite impossible to avoid everything being prepared in advance for a similar evolution and succes-
sion of philosophical systems: just as the road seems to be barred to
certain other possibilities of world interpretation . . . : the spell of
definite grammatical functions is in the last resort the spell of
physiological value judgements and racial conditions . . . (*Beyond
Good and Evil* 20.)

We are prisoners of a grammar invented at an early stage of
human evolution, and it seems that, since we can think only
by using language, our reason too is conditioned by the most
primitive notions of reality: 'Rational thinking is an interpreting according to a scheme which we cannot throw off'. (*The
Will to Power* 522 – note written 1886–7.)

D

Metaphysics: 'the science ... which deals with the fundamental errors of mankind – but as if they were fundamental truths'. (*Human, All Too Human* 18.)

The metaphysical world:

a metaphysical world could exist; the absolute possibility of it can hardly be disputed ... but one can do absolutely nothing with it. ... – For one could assert nothing whatever about it except that it was a being-other, an inaccessible, incomprehensible being-other; it would be a thing with negative qualities. – Even if the existence of such a world were never so well proved, it would be certain that knowledge of it would be the most useless of all forms of knowledge: even more useless than knowledge of the chemical composition of water is to a sailor in danger of shipwreck. (*Human, All Too Human* 9.)

These two early statements provide a concise summary of Nietzsche's lifelong attitude towards metaphysical speculation. The reader of *Twilight of the Idols* will realize that he was a thoroughgoing materialist, and this is not a late development. He in fact derived his materialism from Friedrich Albert Lange's *History of Materialism*, which he read in 1866, when he was twenty. 'Materialism' meant to Lange the absolute inaccessibility of any metaphysical world, the absolute unknowability of anything supra-mundane, the absolute impossibility of saying anything about any world except *this* one. Another world might exist, but we have no way of knowing whether it does so or not: in Kantian terms – which are those Lange used – we can have knowledge only of the phenomenal world (as Kant himself asserted) and therefore anything we know or know about is proved by the fact of our knowing it to be part of the phenomenal world: the noumenal world is, by definition, inaccessible. Nietzsche adopted this view and it became the basic element in his way of thinking. It will be clear that such a form of 'materialism' is not really atheism, although in practice it is indistinguishable from it: Nietzsche assumes in advance that no conception of God can be 'true' because no possibility exists of knowing anything about God, even whether he exists or not. He never asks whether a religious belief, for instance, is true or false, he asks *why* such a belief should be held: and during the course of years his answers to that question become more and more concrete ('materialist'), until by 1888 he is inclined to trace everything back to the *physical condition* of the believer – hence his almost obsessive concern with '*décadence*': for although he still styles himself a psychologist he has grown more and more wary of what one might call the metaphysical element in psychology – all that in it which takes its colouring from the word 'psyche'. Many who would laugh at the suggestion they had a 'soul' are quite certain they possess a 'psyche': this unconscious legerdemain is something against which Nietzsche is guarding when he substitutes 'physiological' for 'psychological' in so many of the formulations of the works of 1888.

The chapter to which this is a note is the most extreme instance of concentrated brevity in all Nietzsche's works. The paradox with which it ends is intended to demonstrate the contradictory and paradoxical nature of all metaphysical philosophy and to assert, although not for the last time, the anti-metaphysical character of his own.

E

Nietzsche's speculations in the field of theory of knowledge are more fragmentary than any other part of his work and most of them remained in unpublished note form. Book Three of *The Will to Power* contains a great many such notes. He was clearly not yet satisfied with his ideas in this field (though neither was he satisfied with any previous epistemological theory). But throughout his published works there can be heard an accent which if we listen to it *can* give us something which might be called 'Nietzsche's epistemology'. It is audible in such statements as the following:

It is the mark of a higher culture to value the little, unpretentious truths which have been discovered by means of rigorous method more highly than the advantageous and dazzling errors which arise in metaphysical and artistic ages and men. (*Human, All Too Human* 3.)
... with religion, art and morality we do not touch upon 'the

nature of the world in itself'; we are in the realm of 'ideas', no 'intuition' can take us any further. (*Human, All Too Human* 10.) The invention of the laws of numbers was based on the primitive, already dominant error that some things are equal to other things (but in fact nothing is equal to anything else), at least that there are things (but there is no 'thing') . . . (*Human, All Too Human* 19.) '*Know thyself*' *is the whole of science*. – Only when man has arrived at knowledge of all things will he have come to know himself. For things are only the boundaries of man. (*Dawn* [1881] 48.)

Let us be on our guard against saying there are laws in nature. There are only necessities: there is no one to command, no one to obey, no one to transgress . . . (*The Gay Science* 109.)

It is not . . . the antithesis of subject and object which concerns me here: I leave this differentiation to the epistemologists, who are caught up in the toils of grammar (the metaphysics of the people). It is even less the antithesis of 'thing in itself' and appearance: for we do not 'know' nearly enough to be permitted so much as to *separate* in this way. For we have no organ whatever for *knowledge*, for 'truth': we 'know' (or believe or fancy) precisely as much as may be *useful* in the interest of the human herd, the species: and even that which is here termed 'usefulness' is only a belief, a fancy, and perhaps precisely that most fatal piece of stupidity through which we shall one day perish. (*The Gay Science* 354.)

There are still harmless self-observers who believe 'immediate certainties' exist, for example 'I think' . . . But I shall reiterate a hundred times that 'immediate certainty', like 'absolute knowledge' and 'thing in itself', contains a *contradictio in adjecto* [contradiction in terms] . . . when I analyse the event expressed in the sentence 'I think' I acquire a series of rash assertions which are difficult, perhaps impossible, to prove – for example, that it is *I* which thinks, that it has to be a something at all which thinks, that thinking is an activity and operation on the part of an entity thought of as a cause, that an 'I' exists, finally that what is designated by 'thinking' has already been determined – that I *know* what thinking is . . . In this way the philosopher acquires in place of that 'immediate certainty' . . . a series of metaphysical questions . . . : 'Whence do I take the concept thinking? Why do I believe in cause and effect? What gives me the right to speak of an I . . . an I as cause . . . an I as cause of thoughts?' . . . (*Beyond Good and Evil* 16.)

There are no certainties and no laws; knowledge of *this* world is full of problems, of any other world impossible; the apparently simplest things turn out on inspection to be enormously complex: this is the tendency of Nietzsche's thoughts on the nature of knowledge. And he insists above all that 'knowledge' is always 'interpretation', that a 'fact' is never something simply seen, it is a mental construct into which a very large number of habits and prejudices enter.

F

No summary, to say nothing of a brief note like this, can do justice to the wealth of psychological insights contained in Nietzsche's works: the works themselves must be read. But one can offer a guide-line by indicating the meaning of his key concepts 'will to power' and 'sublimation'.

'The spiritualization of sensuality is called *love*: it is a great triumph over Christianity'. (*Twilight*, V 3.) Extirpation of sensuality, which Nietzsche alleges is the practice of the Christian Church, is the opposite of its '*Vergeistigung*', of rendering it 'spiritual', which is to say sublimating it. (Nietzsche uses the word '*sublimieren*' and various other words embodying a similar idea, the most frequent of which is '*Selbst-Überwindung*' – self-overcoming: the *Übermensch* (superman) is the 'self-overcome man', the man whose will to power is sublimated.) The concept of sublimation is familiar today through its being part of the vocabulary of psycho-analysis and many references to it in Nietzsche's work also connect the term with sexuality: but to Nietzsche, as is well known, sexuality is not primary – what is primary is the will to power, of which sexuality is an expression; and without going into the question of whether the hypothesis of a will to power is 'true' one can say that the idea of 'sublimated will to power' avoids the objection which can be made to the idea of 'sublimated sexuality' that the supposed object of the drive is annulled in its sublimation and cannot therefore be its actual object. The form of sublimation which Nietzsche noticed first was, in fact, not that of sexuality but of violence: he thought he saw in the Greek games a sublimated form of war; and he soon ventured to suggest that the entire culture of ancient Greece arose from a sublimation of the combative instinct. This interpretation of Greece became famous as an antithesis to the 'sweetness and light' school of thought and has now won general acceptance: at any rate, it is no longer easy to understand how the highly-strung, ferocious and quite naïvely frightful Hellenes could ever have been thought of as embodiments of exalted calm. Now the real innovation in Nietzsche's account of classical civilization lies, not in his having asserted it was actually cruel and bloodthirsty and not at all noble and sublime (which he of course did not assert, although he was misunderstood to have done so), it lies in his contention it was noble and sublime *because* it had been cruel and bloodthirsty. His suggestion was that without these strong passions the culture-creating force would have been lacking. Where did this Greek culture come from? he asked, and answered: It must have come from this original ferocity and blood-lust brought under control. The thought seems to be: where there is 'the sublime' there must have been that which was *made sublime* – sublimated – after having been for a long time not sublime. What he then required was to discover – this is a grand simplification, of course – whether this sub-limating of a 'bad' quality into a 'good' one actually took place in individual human beings: he met Wagner and *saw* it take place – to employ his later terminology, a ferocious will to power was sublimated into the Bayreuth Festival. Every-thing now followed: he began to detect sublimated 'base' impulses in every kind of activity, until he finally ventured the hypothesis that the basic sole drive in man is will to power – 'will' understood, not in any metaphysical sense *à la* Schopenhauer, or as a faculty as in popular psychology, but as a shorthand form for a 'complex of thoughts and feelings and . . . an *emotion*: the emotion of command'. (*Beyond Good and Evil* 19.) (This explains the apparent contradiction between statements in Nietzsche's works containing the word 'will' and his assertion that there is no such thing as will.) Every-thing good proceeds from sublimated 'will to power', every-thing bad from the absence of this 'will' or the absence of sublimation. All the synonyms for 'good' and 'bad' which appear in his later works – 'ascending and declining life', 'life-furthering and life-hostile', 'nobility and *décadence*' – are synonyms for 'adding to the sense of power' and 'subtracting from the sense of power' together with the sublimation or extirpation of this sense.

G

'When I visited men,' says Zarathustra, 'I found them sitting upon an old self-conceit. Each one thought he had long since known what was good and evil for man.' (III 12.) It is his conviction that what is 'good and evil' for man is problematic that lies behind Nietzsche's analysis of morality.

Why is it problematic? Because different peoples have had different moralities: what has been right to one has been wrong to another.

Is it possible to classify these moralities? is a *typology* of morality possible? Yes: there are two basic types: master morality and slave morality – 'I add at once that in all higher and mixed cultures attempts at mediation between the two are apparent and more frequently confusion and mutual mis-understanding between them, and sometimes their harsh juxtaposition – even within the same man, within *one* soul.' (*Beyond Good and Evil* 260.) Master morality arose among a ruling order, slave morality among slaves and dependents: what is 'good' in the former is generally speaking that which permits or expresses the exercise of power, over others and over oneself; what is 'good' in the latter is generally speaking that which protects, comforts and helps. Master morality is positive: the ruling order affirms itself through it and what is not like itself it calls 'bad'; slave morality is negative: it begins with a denial of the morality of the masters and it is after their image that it creates the concept 'evil', as an anti-thesis to which it subsequently creates its concept 'good'. 'Good and bad' belongs to master morality, 'good and *evil*' to slave morality: 'beyond good and evil' therefore does not mean 'beyond good and *bad*'. Master morality arises out of a feeling of power, slave morality out of a feeling of resentment.

Does Nietzsche 'approve' of master morality? Yes, but

only in the way that Freud, for instance, 'approves' of sexuality, that is he does not see it as 'evil'. The contrast between Christian and Hindu morality ('The "Improvers" of Mankind') is instructive here: Nietzsche does not approve of either, though he clearly *prefers* Manu (see also *The Anti-Christ* p. 175). But every morality is false in as much as it posits its own moral valuations as independently valid, as 'morality as such', while these valuations are valid only in so far as they are a means towards the preservation and enhancement of the type of man who holds them: moral 'knowledge' is on all fours with every other kind of knowledge, it is knowledge for use.

H

The meaning of the name 'Dionysus' changes during the course of Nietzsche's works. In the *Birth of Tragedy* it stands for the emotional element in art and life and is the antithesis of 'Apollo', which stands for the form-creating force. (Nietzsche was in fact anticipated by Schelling in introducing the concepts Apollinian and Dionysian into aesthetics, but he may not have known this.) Greek tragedy is conceived of as the result of Apollo's harnessing of Dionysus, and this metaphorical (or mythological) idea is subsequently, in Nietzsche's later works, transformed into a psychological one: Apollo's harnessing of Dionysus then becomes the 'self-overcoming' of the 'animal' man; and since, from *Zarathustra* onwards, Nietzsche recognizes only one force in the human constitution, the will to power, he now calls the entire phenomenon by a single name, that which formerly stood for the emotional forces now subsumed under the rubric 'will to power': 'Dionysus' now means sublimated will to power, and the name is therefore synonymous with *Übermensch*, the man in whom the will to power is sublimated into creativity. The evolution is, in the context of Nietzsche's philosophy, quite logical: but failure to perceive what has happened leads to the familiar accusation of 'inconsistency' because in his first book Nietzsche does not approve of 'Dionysus', while in the works of his last active year he calls himself his 'disciple', and ends his autobiography, *Ecce Homo*, with the challenge: 'Have I been understood? – *Dionysus against the Crucified* . . .'. The best example of the *conceptual* consistency behind the change in the meaning of the name 'Dionysus' is Nietzsche's calling Goethe 'Dionysian'. The epithet most frequently applied to Goethe had always been 'Olympian', meaning among other more complementary things 'cold and aloof'. But in the *Birth of Tragedy* Nietzsche had said that the gods of Olympus were among those Hellenic artistic creations resulting from Apollo's harnessing of Dionysus: thus an 'Olympian man' would in Nietzsche's later terminology necessarily be 'Dionysian'.

GLOSSARY OF NAMES

ARISTOTLE (384–322 B.C.) Nietzsche has only a slight interest in Aristotle, and his main concern with him is to refute his conception of tragedy as catharsis; the 'magnanimous' man of the *Nicomachaean Ethics*, however, is very like Nietzsche's *Übermensch*.

AUGUSTINE (354–430) 'These have mastered Christianity: ... Platonism (Augustine). ...' (*Will to Power* 214); utterly unable to live in the manner of Jesus, Augustine employed Christianity as a vehicle for his *own* ideology in the manner of Paul.

BAUDELAIRE, Charles (1821–67) 'Who was the first *intelligent* supporter of Wagner? Charles Baudelaire. ...' (*Ecce Homo* II 5): Nietzsche's interest in Baudelaire, such as it is, is part of his interest in proving that Wagner was at bottom a French *décadent*.

BORGIA, Cesare (d. 1507) Nietzsche's treatment of Cesare Borgia invites misunderstanding but the invitation should be declined. In *Beyond Good and Evil* (197) he calls him a 'beast of prey' and a 'tropical monster', which are not terms of approbation: but he refuses to agree that such men as he are 'sick' or that the thoroughly domesticated type of man is to be preferred to him. 'Borgia' is an ideogram for the man of strong but unsublimated will to power, the 'blond beast', who is not 'improved' when he is tamed.

BUCKLE, Henry Thomas (1821–62) Historian, author of the unfinished *History of Civilization* in which he expounds his ideas on the general laws which govern the evolution of human societies. His reputation formerly stood much higher than it does now: in the *Genealogy of Morals* (1, 4) Nietzsche attacks the 'plebeianism of the modern spirit' as manifested in the 'notorious case of Buckle'.

BURCKHARDT, Jacob (1818–97) Historian, best known for his *Civilization of the Renaissance in Italy*. He was an elder colleague of Nietzsche's at Basel university and Nietzsche retained a great admiration for him.

CAESAR, Julius (101–44 B.C.) In Nietzsche's works, Caesar is dehistoricized into an ideogram for the man of sublimated will to power (compare Borgia). Nietzsche *does* admire Caesar, but not specifically as a general and certainly not *because* he was a general (compare Napoleon).

CARLYLE, Thomas (1795–1881) In an aphorism in *Dawn* called 'The cult of hero-worship and its fanatics' (298), Nietzsche says of one who idealizes another that he 'sets this person at so great a distance from himself that he can no longer see him clearly – and then he reinterprets what he still sees into the "beautiful", which is to say the symmetrical, soft-lined, indefinite.' The two men he accuses of doing this, Byron and Carlyle, are both as it happens Scotsmen, and it was another Scotsman,

Thomas Campbell, who provided the formula for this kind of perspective in the lines ' 'Tis *distance* lends enchantment to the view, And robes the mountain in its azure hue' and thereby defined a good part of 'Romanticism'. To Nietzsche, Carlyle was a 'typical Romantic'.

CATILINE, Lucius Sergius (c. 109–62 B.C.) Unsuccessful conspiracy against the Senate 63–2 B.C.: his feelings towards that body are likened to Caesar's, his handling of that body contrasted with Caesar's.

COMTE, Auguste (1798–1857) French philosopher, author of the *Cours de philosophie positive* (1830–42). Comte was for Nietzsche the great 'embracer and conqueror of the pure sciences' who at the end of his life allowed his scientific strictness to evaporate into 'poetical mist and mystic lights' (*Dawn* 542).

CORNARO, Luigi (1467–1566) After surviving a nearly fatal illness at forty, he advocated a sparing diet as a recipe for health and long life. 'In later life he found one egg a day sufficient solid food.' (*Encyclopedia Britannica*). His book, *Discorsi sulla vita sobria* (1558), was a best-seller in many languages.

DANTE ALIGHIERI (1265–1321) The scattered references to Dante in Nietzsche's works are highly contradictory and it is obvious he never really came to grips with this poet.

DARWIN, Charles (1809–82) Confrontation with Darwin is a major motif of Nietzsche's philosophy *passim*. There are four main points at issue: (i) in so far as 'Darwinism' means the theory of evolution it is 'true but deadly' because it proves that mankind is a continuation of the animals and that human life is therefore deprived of any special significance; Nietzsche's hypothesis of sublimated will to power is designed to restore a distinction between man and animal; (ii) in so far as Darwinism is the theory of evolution by natural selection brought about by a 'struggle for survival' it is, Nietzsche maintains, untrue, because it presupposes a niggardliness and state of chronic distress in nature which does not exist, the state of nature being on the contrary 'one of superfluity and prodigality, even to the point of absurdity' (*The Gay Science* 349: the unconscious influence on Darwin's theory of the condition of nineteenth century England and of Victorian middle-class thriftiness and money-mindedness in general is now, I think, generally recognized); (iii) in as much as the effects accounted for by the hypothesis of a will to aggrandizement include those accounted for by the hypothesis of a 'will to survive' this latter hypothesis is superfluous; (iv) when a 'struggle for survival' does take place its outcome is not that implied by the theory of natural selection, that is to say it is not a *higher* type which emerges victorious.

DEMOCRITUS (flourished c. 420 B.C.) Greek philosopher, the founder, with Leucippus, of atomism. Nietzsche's attitude towards Democritus' atomism is instructive: he approves of its materialism and of the fact that it can get along without any teleology, but he sees that it is very far from being the complete victory over Parmenides its advocates took it to be: the projection of the notion of a 'subject' from the individual on to the outside world, where it assumes the shape of a 'thing', is certainly not done away with in atomism, for the 'atom' is a 'thing'. The mechanistic idea of atoms as solid objects like billiard balls was instinctively rejected by Nietzsche: and in *Human, All Too Human* (19) he wrote: 'the whole procedure of science has been pursuing the task of resolving everything thing-like (material) into motions.'

DESCARTES, René (1596–1650) In his relatively few references to Descartes, Nietzsche is chiefly concerned to question the validity of Descartes' dictum *cogito, ergo sum,* mainly by way of analysing the proposition 'I think'. This has less to do with Descartes himself than with Nietzsche's general polemic against 'the foisting on of a "subject"'.

DOSTOYEVSKY, Fyodor (1821–81) 'A few weeks ago I did not even know the name of Dostoyevsky. ... A chance reach in a bookshop brought to my notice a work just translated into French, *L'esprit souterrain* [Notes from Underground] ... The instinct of kinship (or what shall I call it?) spoke immediately, my joy was extraordinary: I have to go back to my becoming acquainted with Stendhal's *Rouge et Noir* to recall another such joy.' (Letter of 23 February 1887.) By 7 March he had also read *The House of the Dead* and *The Insulted and Injured,* both likewise in French translation. Whether he read all or any of the four great novels is unknown: in view of his continued enthusiasm for Dostoyevsky his failure to mention any of them in his considerable correspondence of 1887 and 1888 suggests he did not, although one is almost compelled to conclude that the employment of the word 'idiot' to describe Jesus, as well as its rather frequent employment in the works of 1888 in general, derives from a knowledge of Dostoyevsky's *The Idiot*: certainly an awareness of what Dostoyevsky means by that term helps us to understand why Nietzsche should have used it. Since he was twenty-three years younger than Dostoyevsky and produced many of his books after Dostoyevsky was dead, it is important to note how late it was before he came to read him: what suggests Dostoyevsky in Nietzsche's writings before 1887 is not the product of influence or borrowing but of a similarity in psychological acumen.

ELIOT, George (Mary Ann Evans, 1819–80) Nietzsche's friend Helene Druscowicz was a great admirer of George Eliot, wrote about her and talked to Nietzsche about her. Fräulein Druscowicz could read English (she translated Swinburne into German), Nietzsche could not, or only very haltingly, and it seems likely he knew of George Eliot mainly from her: he clearly thought of Eliot mainly as an English free-thinker. The reference to her in *Twilight* is the only one in Nietzsche's works.

EMERSON, Ralph Waldo (1803–82) Aphorism 92 of *The Gay Science,* on the relation between poetry and prose, names the only four 'masters of prose' of the nineteenth century (Goethe being considered a product of the eighteenth): Leopardi, Mérimée, Emerson and Landor. Whatever one may think of this judgement, and of its somewhat narrow conception of what constitutes good prose, it provides evidence of Nietzsche's extreme admiration for Emerson. The original edition of *The Gay Science* (1882) is prefaced by a quotation from Emerson, and he admired Emerson longer and with greater consistency than he did any other contemporary writer: his holiday programme for 1862 included making extracts from *all* Emerson's essays (no record of whether he actually did so) and his enthusiasm is just as great in 1888.

EPICURUS (341–270 B.C.) Greek philosopher, adopted the physics and the ethical teaching of Democritus and made of the latter the influential moral doctrine named after him. For Nietzsche, 'the garden god' Epicurus is a mood rather than a man: aphorism 295 of *The Wanderer and his Shadow*, in which Epicurus is called 'one of the greatest human beings, the inventor of an heroic-idyllic mode of philosophizing', is a description of this mood.

FONTENELLE, Bernard Le Bovier de (1657–1757) French writer. He appears here as a representative of the group of six – the others are Montaigne, La Rochefoucauld, La Bruyère, Vauvenargues and Chamfort – of whom Nietzsche says (*Wanderer and his Shadow* 214) that one is closer to antiquity when reading them than with any similar group of any other nation: 'Their books . . . contain more *actual ideas* than all the books of German philosophers put together.'

FRIEDRICH THE SECOND (1194–1250) King of Sicily from 1198, king of Germany from 1212, 'emperor of the West' from 1220; continually in conflict with the Papacy; although excommunicated he took part in the sixth crusade, when he negotiated with the Mohammedans instead of fighting them and gained the city of Jerusalem without bloodshed. His court in Sicily was possibly the most cultured spot in Europe, and Friedrich himself, although the 'German Christian emperor', was more of a Mohammedan than a Christian and more of an Italian than a German. The need to be continually on the defensive against the forces of the Pope produced a deterioration in his character in later years which ended in a species of persecution mania. Nietzsche's admiration for him is unqualified and it is interesting to see why: 'the *first* European according to my taste' (*Beyond Good and Evil* 200) he calls him at the end of a discussion of the possibility that higher types of men are produced as a consequence of racial mixture: it is Friedrich's cosmopolitan culture which Nietzsche admires, the 'good European'. (In expressing his admiration for Friedrich the *Second* Nietzsche is probably also expressing his lack of admiration for the traditionally admired Friedrich the *First*, called Barbarossa.)

GOETHE, Johann Wolfgang (1749–1832) The modern man Nietzsche admired most and the one who provided him with a yardstick against which he measured the achievements of other men; a type of the *Übermensch* or 'Dionysian man'. The description of Goethe in

'Expeditions of an Untimely Man' 49 defines the *Übermensch* more succinctly than any other single passage in Nietzsche's works.

GONCOURT, Edmond (1822–96) and Jules (1830–70) French writers of the naturalist school. 'The second volume of the *Journal des Goncourts* has appeared . . . in it are described in the most vivid way the celebrated *dîners chez Magny*, those dinners which brought together every fortnight the wittiest and most sceptical company of Parisian spirits of the time (Sainte-Beuve, Flaubert, Théophile Gautier, Taine, Renan, the Goncourts, Schérer, Gavarni, occasionally Turgenev, etc.). Exasperated pessimism, cynicism, nihilism, alternating with much boisterousness and good humour; I myself wouldn't be at all out of place there – I know these gentlemen inside out, *so well* that I have really had enough of them already. One has to be more radical: fundamentally they all lack the main thing – "*la force*". (Letter of 10 November 1887.)

HARTMANN, Eduard von (1842–1906) German philosopher, author of *Philosophy of the Unconscious*. Often referred to by Nietzsche, always with contempt.

HEGEL, Georg Wilhelm Friedrich (1770–1831) Nietzsche's relation to Hegel is complex and cannot be satisfactorily described in a note. Two things can be noted, however: (i) Nietzsche's basic attitude towards Hegel was that his philosophy was the conceptual basis of modern 'evolutionism' and thus encouraged a habit of mind which ought to be deprecated; (ii) Nietzsche clearly did not study Hegel very profoundly and was in many ways closer to him than he suspected, although he acknowledged that 'we Germans would be Hegelians even if Hegel had never existed, in as much as we instinctively accord a profounder significance and a greater value to becoming and evolution than we do to that which "is" . . . .' (*The Gay Science* 357.)

HEINE, Heinrich (1797–1856) German-Jewish poet and writer. 'The highest conception of the lyric poet was given me by *Heinrich Heine*. I seek in vain in all the realms of the millennia for an equally sweet and passionate music. He possessed that divine malice without which I cannot conceive the perfect. – I estimate the value of human beings, of races, according to how necessarily they do not know how to understand the god apart from the satyr. – And how he handles German! It will one day be said that Heine and I have been by far the greatest artists of the German language . . . ' (*Ecce Homo* II 4.)

HERACLITUS (c. 500 B.C.) Greek philosopher. Because of his dynamic view of nature much admired by Nietzsche. In his pride and isolation, and the sibylline character of his utterances, he is the ultimate model for Zarathustra.

HORACE (Quintus Horatius Flaccus, 65–8 B.C.) Often quoted by Nietzsche, although sometimes the quotations are only familiar tags, e.g. *aere perennius*.

HUGO, Victor (1802–85) 'Victor Hugo and Richard Wagner – they signify one and the same thing: that in declining cultures, that wherever the decision comes to rest with the masses, genuineness becomes super-fluous, disadvantageous, an encumbrance. Only the actor still arouses *great* enthusiasm.' (*The Wagner Case* 11.)

KANT, Emmanuel (1724–1804) There are scores of references to Kant in Nietzsche's works, and the greater part of them are hostile. What Nietzsche held against Kant can, however, be stated in a single sentence: that Kant believed in and sought to demonstrate the existence of a 'moral world-order'.

LEIBNIZ, Gottfried Wilhelm (1646–1716) Nietzsche credits Leibniz with and praises him for the discovery that 'what we call consciousness constitutes only a condition of our spiritual and psychical world (perhaps a morbid condition) and is *very far from constituting this world itself*'. (*The Gay Science* 357): the connexion with Nietzsche's speculations will be clear. Otherwise he has little interest in Leibniz.

LISZT, Franz (1811–86), 'who excels all other musicians in the nobility of his orchestral tone' (*Ecce Homo* II 7) – but because he was Wagner's father-in-law Nietzsche cannot resist making jokes about him. Liszt was, of course, very much an 'actor' in Nietzsche's sense of the word.

LOBECK, Christian August (1781–1860) German philologist and anti-quary; a specialist in the history of the Greek language. He wrote many scholarly works.

LUTHER, Martin (1483–1546) The long polemic in *The Anti-Christ* against 'faith' as the distinguishing characteristic of the Christian expresses what lies behind Nietzsche's long-standing enmity towards Luther: emphasis on 'faith' is merely a confession of incapacity for 'works'. Nietzsche also continually emphasizes Luther's coarseness and his enmity towards reason.

MACHIAVELLI, Niccolo (1469–1527) Admired by Nietzsche for his 'realism'; but Nietzsche refers to him very infrequently and there seems no good reason for linking their names as is sometimes done.

MALTHUS, Thomas Robert (1766–1834) 'Population, when unchecked, increases in a geometrical ratio. Subsistence only increases in an arith-metical ratio . . . the power of population is indefinitely greater than the power in the earth to produce subsistence for man.' (*Essay on the Prin-ciple of Population* [1798].)

MICHELET, Jules (1798–1874) Historian of France and of the Revolu-tion. Nietzsche links him with Schiller and Carlyle as an idealizing historian. (*Will to Power* 343.)

MILL, John Stuart (1806–73) Very few references to Mill in Nietzsche's works, but many hostile ones to 'utilitarianism', which was especially Mill's ethical theory.

NAPOLEON BONAPARTE (1769–1821) Not, despite occasional sugges-tions to the contrary, a type of the *Übermensch,* but a 'synthesis of *Unmensch* [monster] and *Übermensch*' (*Genealogy of Morals* I 16) – that is to say, a 'problem'. Nietzsche worries this problem of Napoleon from the beginning of his life till the end, but arrives at no definite conclusion.

Many of his statements about Napoleon are neutral as regards 'admiration' or 'dislike': they seek to *describe*. He shows no interest in his military campaigns and his assessment of him does not involve consideration of his generalship.

PASCAL, Blaise (1623–62)   French mathematician and philosopher. At the age of sixteen he wrote a treatise on conic sections and at eighteen invented a computer; later he invented, among other things, the calculus of probability and the hydraulic press. On the night of 23 November 1654 he suffered a mystical 'conversion' to religious belief and from then on frequented Port-Royal and devoted himself largely to religious controversy and to introspective philosophizing and meditation (his celebrated *Pensées*). Nietzsche mentions Pascal dozens of times, and always with reference to this religious conversion and its consequences: he is 'the most instructive of all sacrifices to Christianity'. (*Ecce Homo* II 3.)

PETRONIUS, Caius (suicide A.D. 65)   Author of the *Satyricon*, a satire in prose and verse on the social life of first century Rome.

PLATO (428–347 B.C.)   'Plato *against* Homer: that is the whole, the genuine antagonism' (*Genealogy of Morals* III 25): the former as a slanderer of life, the latter as its glorifier. Nietzsche's attitude becomes comprehensible in the light of his own 'materialism', for in that light Plato becomes a falsifier of reality. Nietzsche considered Plato's theory of suprasensible forms, his ethical preoccupation and his other-worldly tendency in general as harmful to a healthy appreciation of the present world and as specific errors springing from a false relationship with the actual world: Plato is one of those who need to 'lie themselves out of reality'.

RENAN, Ernest (1823–92)   French rationalist writer: the type of the freethinker who has not really freed himself from religion.

ROUSSEAU, Jean-Jacques (1712–78)   In his essay *Schopenhauer as an Educator* (the third of the *Untimely Meditations*, 1874), Nietzsche offers a comparison between Rousseau and Goethe, the former representing the revolutionary man and the latter the contemplative, and in 'Expeditions of an Untimely Man' 48 and 49 he contrasts them again. Goethe is now, of course, much more than the contemplative man: he is, in fact, the superman, the embodiment of sublimated will to power; and Rousseau too has undergone a change, this time for the worse: from the revolutionary he has declined to the rabble, and is in fact the representative of *unsublimated* will to power. Nietzsche's long polemic against Rousseau – there are dozens of references to him – can best be understood in the light of this symbolism: Rousseau's 'back to nature' means back to the animals, back to passion *uncontrolled*.

SAINT-SIMON, Claude-Henri, Comte de (1760–1825)   Inventor of an economic theory involving common ownership of property and distribution of goods: the Saint-Simonians acquired rather quickly some of the characteristics of religious fanaticism.

SAINTE-BEUVE, Charles-Augustin (1804–69) Very influential literary critic and historian. Nietzsche criticizes, here and elsewhere, his celebrated 'objectivity'.

SALLUST (86–c.35 B.C.) Latin historian; chronicled the Catiline conspiracy. He modelled his style on that of Thucydides.

SAND, George (Aurore Dupin, Baroness Dudevant, 1804–76) Novelist and writer. 'It betrays corruption of the instincts – quite apart from the fact that it betrays bad taste – when a woman appeals precisely to Madame Roland or Madame de Staël or Monsieur George Sand as if something *in favour* of "woman as such" were thereby demonstrated. Among men the above-named are the three *comic* women as such – nothing more! – and precisely the best involuntary *counter-arguments* against emancipation and female autocracy.' (*Beyond Good and Evil* 233.)

SCHILLER, Friedrich (1759–1805) As a youth Nietzsche was a Schiller enthusiast; he lost his enthusiasm as he grew older. From that he concluded that Schiller was essentially something for young people (this opinion is expressed several times in his works). Ultimately he considered Schiller superficial and Romantic.

SCHOPENHAUER, Arthur (1788–1860) His *World as Will and Idea* (1818) was a major influence on the young Nietzsche, who for many years considered himself a 'Schopenhaueran': but Schopenhauer's pessimism, his duality of will and intellect, his metaphysical preoccupation and his hostility towards the emotions, particularly sexuality, were none of them finally acceptable and Nietzsche's mature philosophy is not indebted to Schopenhauer in any way. His youthful discipleship is, however, the reason for the frequency with which the older Nietzsche makes polemical points against Schopenhauer.

SOCRATES (470–399 B.C.) 'Socrates ... stands so close to me that I am almost always fighting with him', Nietzsche confessed in the notes for an uncompleted essay of 1875 (*Wissenschaft und Weisheit im Kampfe*) and the fight went on until the end. Socrates is the type of 'the philosopher' and in investigating the mind and heart of Socrates Nietzsche is investigating his own: with none of the figures he discusses is the tremendous inner dialectic of Nietzsche's lifelong monologue so clearly displayed as it is in the passages dealing with Socrates (of which there are hundreds). The 'problem' of Socrates is the problem of reason, of the status of reason in the life of man: and Nietzsche finds that problem inexhaustible.

SPENCER, Herbert (1820–1903) Philosopher of evolution. Nietzsche never refers to him without disdain.

SPINOZA, Baruch (1632–77) On five main points, Nietzsche says in a letter of 30 July 1881, he finds that he and Spinoza are in agreement: on denying free will, purpose, the moral world-order, the unegoistic and the existence of evil. But he deprecates 'that hocus-pocus of mathematical form with which Spinoza encased his philosophy as if in brass'. (*Beyond Good and Evil* 5.)

STENDHAL (Henri Beyle, 1783–1842)   Greatly admired by Nietzsche for his psychological insight and as an *honest* atheist . . . Perhaps I am even envious of Stendhal? He has robbed me of the best atheist joke, which precisely I could have made: "God's only excuse is that he does not exist." ' (*Ecce Homo* II 3.)

STRAUSS, David (1808–74)   His *Life of Jesus* and *The Old Faith and the New* were very popular expositions of the rationalist approach to religion. The first of Nietzsche's *Untimely Meditations – David Strauss, the Confessor and the Writer* (1873) – was a violent attack on him.

THUCYDIDES (c. 460–c. 395 B.C.)   Greek historian, author of the *History of the Peloponnesian War*.

TOLSTOY, Leo (1828–1910)   *Décadent* because of his emphasis on 'pity'. (*Genealogy of Morals* III 26, *Will to Power* 1020.) That 'resist not evil' is the key to the Gospel may have been suggested to Nietzsche by Tolstoy (see Tolstoy's *My Religion*, chapter 1), but the conclusions he draws from this have nothing to do with Tolstoy.

WAGNER, Richard (1813–83)   As a youth Nietzsche was deeply under Wagner's influence; around 1876 he broke away, but the figure of Wagner continued to haunt him and there is an unceasing dialogue between the two in Nietzsche's works almost *passim*. In the mature Nietzsche, Wagner is the type of 'the artist'. He plays a relatively minor role in *Twilight* because an entire book, *The Wagner Case*, had just been devoted to him; but later in the year 1888 he comes to the forefront again in *Nietzsche contra Wagner*.

WINCKELMANN, Johann Joachim (1717–68)   Archaeologist and historian of art whose conception of ancient Greece became the accepted one for the German world throughout the eighteenth century. Goethe's view of the ancient world derived from Winckelmann, whose writings he studied and whom he celebrated in *Winckelmann and his Century* (1805).

ZOLA, Emile (1840–1902)   'There is no such thing as pessimistic art. . . . Art affirms. Job affirms. – But Zola? But the Goncourts? – The things they exhibit are ugly: but *that* they exhibit them comes from *pleasure in this ugliness*. . . .' (*Will to Power* 821.)